FUN-SIZE QUILTS

17 POPULAR DESIGNERS PLAY
WITH FAT QUARTERS

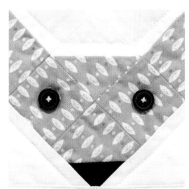

Compiled by Karen M. Burns

Martingale®
Create with Confidence

Fun-Size Quilts:
17 Popular Designers Play with Fat Quarters
© 2014 by Martingale & Company®

Martingale®
19021 120th Ave. NE, Ste. 102
Bothell, WA 98011-9511 USA
ShopMartingale.com

Printed in China
19 18 17 16 15 14   8 7 6 5 4 3 2 1

Library of Congress Cataloging-in-Publication Data is available upon request.

ISBN: 978-1-60468-419-3

MISSION STATEMENT
Dedicated to providing quality products and service to inspire creativity.

CREDITS
PRESIDENT AND CEO: Tom Wierzbicki
EDITOR IN CHIEF: Mary V. Green
DESIGN DIRECTOR: Paula Schlosser
MANAGING EDITOR: Karen Costello Soltys
ACQUISITIONS EDITOR: Karen M. Burns
TECHNICAL EDITOR: Laurie Baker
COPY EDITOR: Melissa Bryan
PRODUCTION MANAGER: Regina Girard
COVER AND INTERIOR DESIGNER: Adrienne Smitke
PHOTOGRAPHER: Brent Kane
ILLUSTRATOR: Missy Shepler

Contents

Introduction

Petite, diminutive, wee, fun-size: all words that suggest small and adorable, like the quilts in this book.

Small quilts can be quick and easy, made up of strips and squares, or they can feature more complex design and construction. Working at a small scale means you can whip up a last-minute gift, or break out of the routine and create something unexpected, just for the fun of it.

We invited a talented group of designers to challenge themselves to keep it small. We asked them to create a quilt that was no bigger than a fat quarter, and they responded with enthusiasm and this collection of fabulous designs.

The 19 projects represent a range of styles, from bold prints and graphic lines to cheerful flowers and sweet woodland creatures. One quilt features a message hidden in Morse code! Choose a project that uses your favorite technique or try something new. From traditional pieced blocks to easygoing strip piecing, English paper piecing, and simple appliqué, there are lots of options. What all the projects have in common, besides their size, is an undeniable freshness and charm that makes them irresistible.

So go ahead, pick a project and join the fun. Make two, they're small!

"To-Do List," designed and made by Debbie Grifka, Esch House Quilts

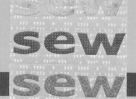
To-Do List

Sometimes my to-do lists make me feel overwhelmed, but not this one! This little quilt hangs in my sewing room to remind me that sometimes you just have to do what you have to do!

~Debbie

MATERIALS

Yardage is based on 42"-wide fabric unless otherwise noted. Fat quarters are approximately 18" x 21".

½ yard OR 2 fat quarters of yellow print for background and facing

Scraps, approximately 3" x 12" *each*, of 3 assorted prints for letter appliqués

2½" x 21" strip of gray print for "stitches"

⅝ yard of fabric for backing

19" x 22" piece of batting

¼ yard of 17"-wide fusible web

¼ yard of 18"-wide stabilizer (optional)

CUTTING

For all cutting, place the shortest edge of the fabric along the bottom edge of the cutting mat.

From the yellow print, cut:

1 square, 14¾" x 14¾"

1 strip, 2¾" x 14¾"

1 strip, 5¾" x 14¾"

1 rectangle, 2¾" x 5¾"

4 strips, 1½" x 21"

From the gray 2½" x 21" strip, crosscut:

2 rectangles, 1" x 2½"; set aside the remainder for the strip set

APPLIQUÉING THE QUILT TOP

1. Trace the letter patterns on page 10 onto the paper side of the fusible web three times each, leaving approximately ½" between shapes. Cut out each letter about ¼" outside of the traced lines.

2. Follow the manufacturer's instructions to fuse one *s*, one *e*, and one *w* to the wrong side of each of the three assorted-print scraps. Cut out each letter on the traced lines, and remove the paper backing.

3. Position each letter on the right side of the yellow 14¾" square as shown to spell the word *sew* three times. Refer to the diagram for placement and center the middle word between the top and bottom words.

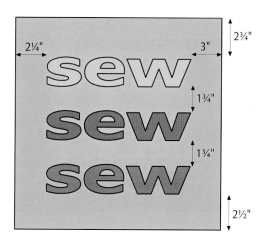

4. Stitch the letters in place using a narrow, slightly open zigzag stitch; use the stabilizer beneath the yellow fabric, if desired. The sample quilt was made with the stitch width set at 3.0 and the length set at 1.0.

ASSEMBLING THE QUILT TOP

Press all seam allowances toward the gray print.

1. Sew a yellow 1½" x 21" strip to the remainder of the gray 2½"-wide strip along the long edges to make a strip set. Crosscut the strip set into 11 segments, 1" wide.

Make 1.
Cut 11 segments.

2. Alternating fabrics, sew five of the segments from step 1 together end to end to make the horizontal row of "stitching"; press. Sew six segments together to make the vertical row of stitching; press. Sew a gray 1" x 2½" rectangle to the end of each row so that both rows begin and end with gray fabric; press.

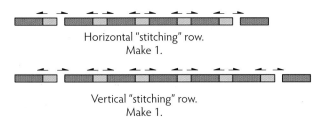

Horizontal "stitching" row.
Make 1.

Vertical "stitching" row.
Make 1.

3. Cut the vertical row of stitching apart through the center of the fifth yellow rectangle. With the raw edges aligned, sew the longer portion of the trimmed vertical stitching row to the right edge of the appliquéd section as shown; press. Set aside the shorter section for use later. Sew the yellow 2¾" x 14¾" strip to the right edge of this unit; press.

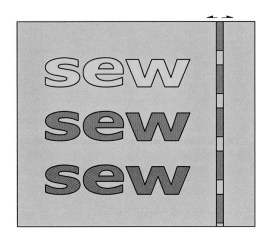

4. Sew the horizontal row of stitching from step 2 to the bottom edge of the appliquéd unit from step 3; press.

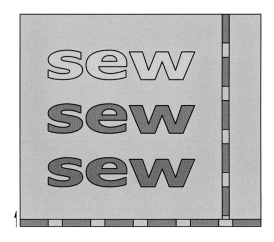

5. Sew the trimmed piece from step 3 between the yellow 5¾" x 14¾" strip and the yellow 2¾" x 5¾" rectangle; press. Sew this completed section to the bottom of the quilt top; press. The quilt top should measure 17½" x 20½".

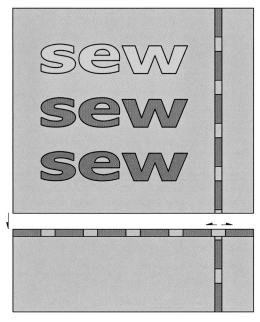

Quilt assembly

FINISHING THE QUILT

For help with any of the finishing techniques, go to ShopMartingale.com/HowtoQuilt to download free how-to information.

1. Layer the quilt top with backing and batting; baste the layers together.

2. Quilt as desired. The featured quilt is machine quilted with horizontal lines.

3. Press under ¼" on one long edge of each of the four yellow 1½" x 21" facing strips. With the raw edges aligned, stitch a facing strip to each long side of the quilt top.

4. Press the facing to the back of the quilt along the seam line. Hand stitch the strips in place along the folded edges.

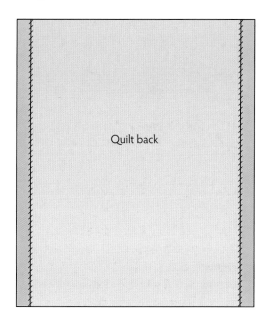

Quilt back

5. Center and sew the remaining two facing strips to the top and bottom edges of the quilt top. Trim the excess from the facing strips, leaving an extra ¼" on each end. Press the facing to the back of the quilt along the seam line. Press under the short raw ends of each facing strip ¼" and stitch the facing in place along the folded edges.

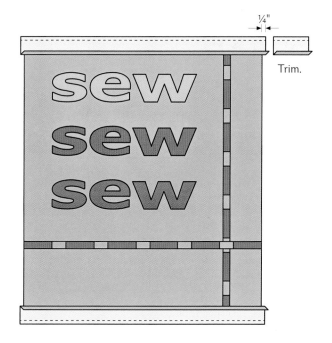

¼"

Trim.

Appliqué patterns do not include seam allowance. Patterns have been reversed for fusible appliqué.

Put a new spin on the basic four-patch unit by mixing it with squares and rectangles for a simple but interesting block. Choose floral prints in an array of bold colors to keep the mood fresh and lively.

~Julie

MATERIALS

Yardage is based on 42"-wide fabric. Fat quarters are approximately 18" x 21".

Scraps, approximately 5" x 6" *each*, of 16 assorted prints for blocks

⅛ yard of yellow print for block four-patch units

⅛ yard of purple print for block four-patch units

⅛ yard of green print for single-fold binding

1 fat quarter of fabric for backing

15" x 19" piece of batting

CUTTING

From the yellow print, cut:
3 strips, 1" x 42"

From the purple print, cut:
3 strips, 1" x 42"

From *each* of the 16 assorted-print scraps, cut:
3 rectangles, 1½" x 2½" (48 total)
3 squares, 1½" x 1½" (48 total)

From the green print, cut:
2 strips, 1¼" x 42"

MAKING THE BLOCKS

1. Sew a yellow strip to a purple strip along the long edges to make a strip set. Repeat to make a total of three strip sets. Press the seam allowances open. Crosscut the strip sets into 96 segments, 1" wide.

Make 3.
Cut 96 segments.

2. Sew two segments from step 1 together as shown to make a four-patch unit. Press the seam allowances open. Repeat to make a total of 48 units.

Make 48.

3. Sew a four-patch unit to an assorted-print square, making sure to orient the four-patch unit as shown. Press the seam allowances open.

4. Sew a matching assorted-print rectangle to the bottom of the unit from step 3 as shown. Press the seam allowances open.

5. Repeat steps 3 and 4 to make a total of 48 blocks.

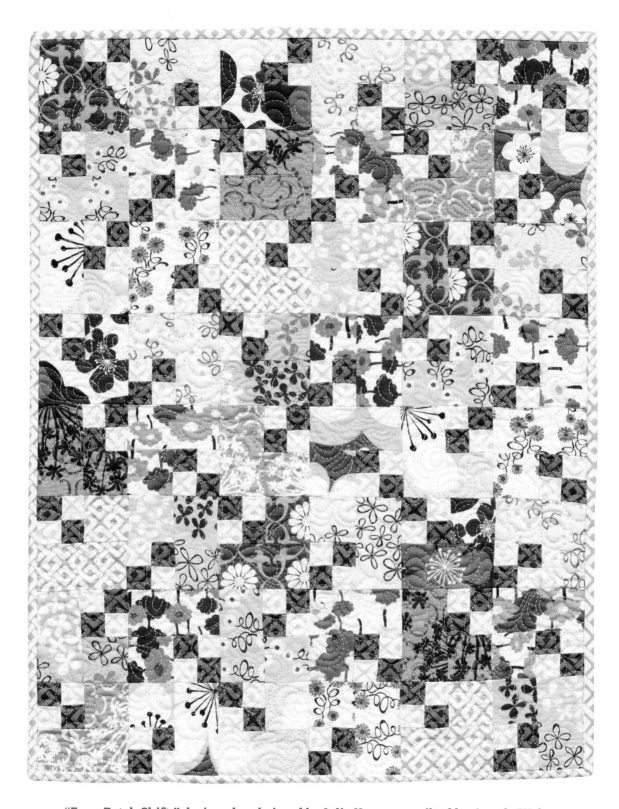

"Four-Patch Shift," designed and pieced by Julie Herman; quilted by Angela Walters

ASSEMBLING THE QUILT TOP

1. Refer to the quilt assembly diagram to lay out the blocks in eight rows of six blocks each, rotating the blocks as shown so that the odd-numbered rows have four-patch units alternating between the top right and bottom right and the even-numbered rows have four-patch units alternating between the top left and bottom left.

2. Sew the blocks in each row together. Press the seam allowances open. Sew the rows together. Press the seam allowances open.

FINISHING THE QUILT

For help with any of the finishing techniques, go to ShopMartingale.com/HowtoQuilt to download free how-to information.

1. Layer the quilt top with backing and batting; baste the layers together.

2. Quilt as desired.

3. Sew the green 1¼"-wide strips together at right angles to make one long strip. Press the seam allowances open. Press under one long raw edge ¼".

4. With the raw edges aligned, stitch the binding strip to the quilt edges in the same manner as you would for double-fold binding, mitering the corners. Fold the binding to the quilt back and stitch the folded edge in place.

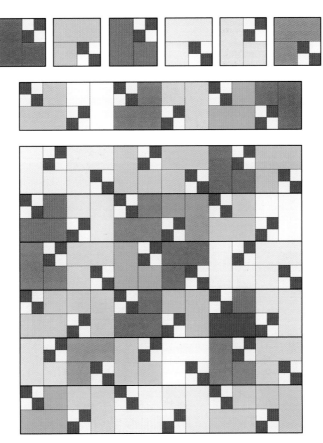

Quilt assembly

"Quiltilicious," designed and made by Melissa Corry

> illed with lots of movement, bright colors, and a great geometric design, this mesmerizing mini will be the perfect wall hanging for your special space.
>
> ~Melissa

MATERIALS

Yardage is based on 42"-wide fabric. Fat quarters are approximately 18" x 21".

1 fat quarter *each* of red, pink, purple, and gray prints*

¼ yard of black solid for binding

⅔ yard of fabric for backing

21" x 21" piece of batting

*See "Color Placement" below if you'd like to substitute colors.

Color Placement

If you'd like to tell your own color story, choose four colors—two colors for the focal squares (red and purple), one color for the center lattice (pink), and one color for the side lattice (gray).

CUTTING

From *each* of the red and purple prints, cut:
14 squares, 3" x 3" (28 total)

From the pink print, cut:
4 strips, 1½" x 18"
6 squares, 1½" x 1½"
28 rectangles, 1½" x 2½"

From the gray print, cut:
4 strips, 1½" x 18"
6 squares, 1½" x 1½"
26 rectangles, 1½" x 2½"

From the black solid, cut:
2 strips, 2½" x 42"

MAKING THE HALF-SQUARE-TRIANGLE UNITS

1. Draw a diagonal line from corner to corner on the wrong side of each red 3" square.

2. Place a marked square on a purple 3" square, right sides together. Stitch ¼" from both sides of the marked line. Cut the squares apart on the marked line to make two half-square-triangle units. Press the seam allowances open. Repeat to make a total of 28 units. Trim each half-square-triangle unit to measure 2½" x 2½".

Make 28.

MAKING THE LATTICE UNITS

1. Sew a pink 1½" x 18" strip to a gray 1½" x 18" strip along the long edges to make a strip set. Press the seam allowances toward the gray strip. Repeat to make a total of four strip sets. Crosscut the strip sets into 24 segments, 2½" wide.

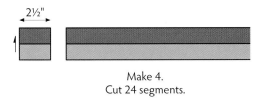

Make 4.
Cut 24 segments.

2. Sew pink and gray rectangles to each segment from step 1 as shown. Press the seam allowances toward the rectangles.

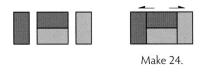

Make 24.

3. Sew a pink 1½" square to a gray 1½" square. Press the seam allowances toward the gray square. Repeat to make a total of six units.

Make 6.

4. Sew the units from step 3 to the remaining pink and gray 1½" x 2½" rectangles as shown. Press the seam allowances toward the rectangles.

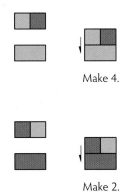

Make 4.

Make 2.

ASSEMBLING THE QUILT TOP

1. Refer to the quilt assembly diagram to arrange the half-square-triangle units and lattice units in nine vertical rows, being careful to orient each unit correctly to form the pattern. You will have one half-square-triangle unit left over.

2. Sew the units in each row together. Press the seam allowances toward the lattice units. Sew the rows together. Press the seam allowances open.

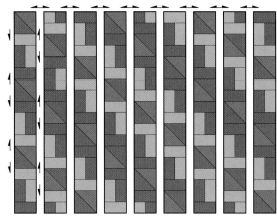

Quilt assembly

FINISHING THE QUILT

For help with any of the finishing techniques, go to ShopMartingale.com/HowtoQuilt to download free how-to information.

1. Layer the quilt top with backing and batting; baste the layers together.

2. Quilt as desired.

3. Bind the quilt edges using the black 2½"-wide strips.

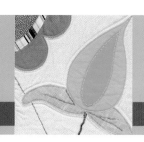

The modern design of this mini-quilt allows the colorful fabrics to shine, while giving you a chance to explore different appliqué and hand-embroidery techniques.

~Heather

MATERIALS

Yardage is based on 42"-wide fabric unless otherwise noted. Fat quarters are approximately 18" x 21".

⅛ yard *each* of orange solid, purple solid, bright-pink mini-dot print, bright-pink dash print, light-turquoise solid, dark-turquoise solid, and green print for flower and leaf appliqués

1 fat quarter of small-scale light print for background

1 fat quarter of multicolored stripe for flower appliqué and binding

⅔ yard of fabric for backing

⅔ yard of batting

1¾ yards of 1.5 mm dark-green rattail cord for stems

½ yard of 20"-wide paper-backed fusible web

Thread to match or contrast with appliqués

Green and black 6-strand embroidery floss

Bright-pink and bright-blue 4-ply cotton yarn for embroidery

Size 18 chenille needle

Fabric marking pen

CUTTING

From the bright-pink mini-dot print, cut:
1 rectangle, 5" x 9"

From the batting, cut:
1 rectangle, 20" x 23"
1 rectangle, 6" x 10"

From the multicolored stripe, cut:
1 square, 16" x 16"; cut into 2½"-wide bias strips. Set aside the remainder for the appliqué.

APPLIQUÉING THE QUILT TOP

1. Trace the patterns on pages 20–23 onto the paper side of the fusible web, leaving approximately ½" between shapes. Roughly cut out each shape. Follow the manufacturer's instructions to fuse each shape to the appropriate fabric. Cut out each shape on the traced lines, and remove the paper backing.

2. Trim the light-print fat quarter to 18" x 21" if necessary. Lay the rectangle on your work surface, right side up, with the short edges at the top and bottom and the long edges at the sides. Position the daisy petals appliqué on the upper-left corner of the rectangle, aligning the straight ends of the daisy petals with the top and left edges of the rectangle. *Do not* fuse the appliqué in place. Using the fabric marker, trace the inner curve of the petals onto the rectangle. Remove the appliqué.

3. Center the light-print rectangle over the large batting rectangle, right side up. Sandwich the pink 5" x 9" rectangle between the batting and the light-print rectangles in the upper-left corner, aligning the fabric raw edges. Place the 6" x 10" batting rectangle under all three layers in the upper-left corner. Stitch on the marked line.

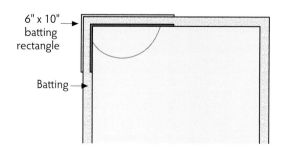

6" x 10" batting rectangle

Batting

"Garden Variety," designed and made by Heather Valentine

4. Carefully trim away the light fabric above the stitching line to expose the pink fabric. Trim away the excess batting below the stitching line, close to the stitching.

5. Following the manufacturer's instructions and referring to the photo (page 18) as necessary, position and fuse the daisy petals shape to the upper-left corner of the light rectangle, matching the curve of the pink fabric. Using matching or contrasting thread and a straight stitch, stitch close to the scalloped edges. Position the daisy band so that it covers the inner curve of the petals and the outer curve of the pink center, and then straight stitch it in place along the inner and outer curved edges.

6. Refer to the appliqué placement guide to position and fuse the remaining appliqués in place. Using a straight stitch and matching or contrasting thread, stitch along the edges of each piece.

Appliqué placement

ADDING THE EMBROIDERY DETAILS

1. Using the fabric marking pen, freehand draw the flower stem lines and leaf detail lines, referring to the photo as necessary.

2. Using six strands of green floss and the chenille needle, backstitch the leaf detail lines and daisy stem line.

Backstitch

3. Position and pin the rattail cord in place over the tulip and crocus stem lines, using three separate pieces for the crocus. Using six strands of black floss and the chenille needle, couch the cord in place.

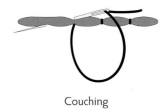

Couching

4. Using the chenille needle and alternating pink and blue yarn, make French knots along the stem of the crocus.

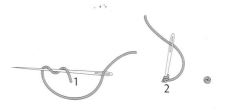

French knot

FINISHING THE QUILT

For help with any of the finishing techniques, go to ShopMartingale.com/HowtoQuilt to download free how-to information.

1. Layer the quilt top and batting sandwich with backing; baste the layers together.

2. Quilt as desired.

3. Sew the multicolored bias strips together at right angles to make one long strip, and use the strip to bind the quilt edges.

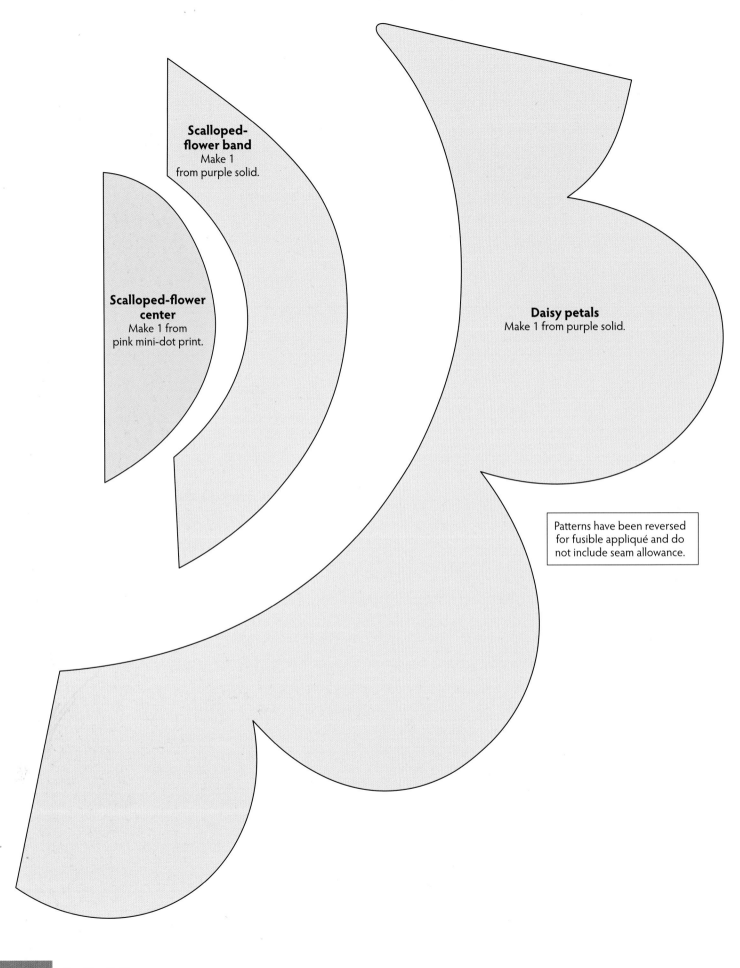

Scalloped-flower band
Make 1
from purple solid.

Scalloped-flower center
Make 1 from
pink mini-dot print.

Daisy petals
Make 1 from purple solid.

Patterns have been reversed
for fusible appliqué and do
not include seam allowance.

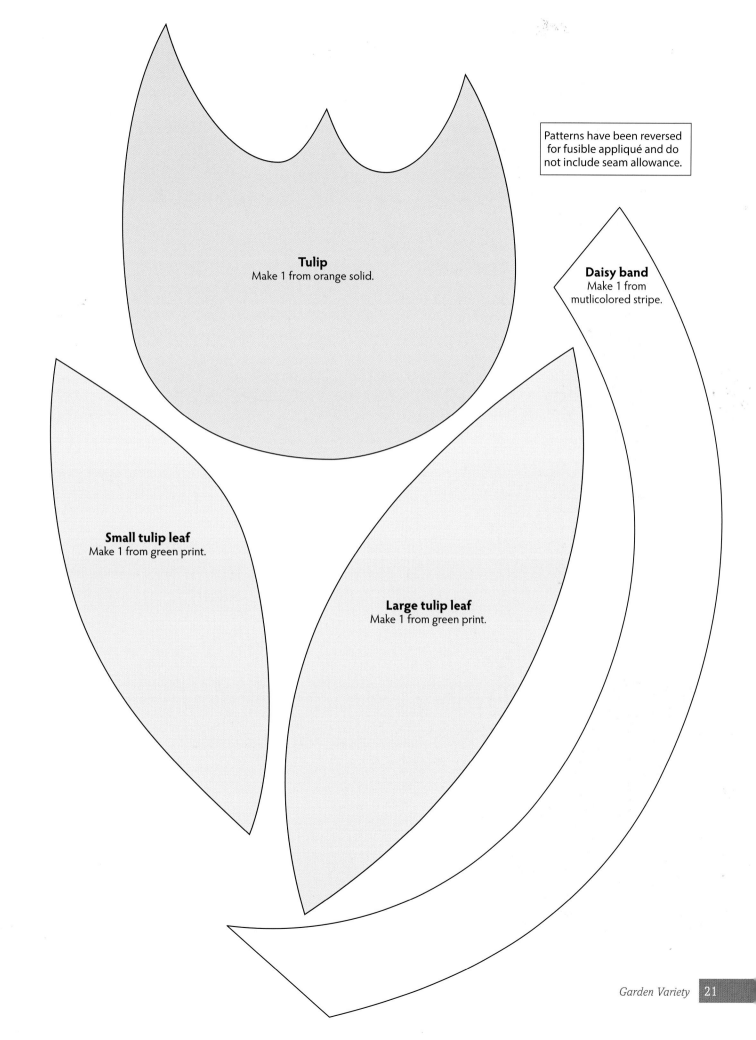

Tulip
Make 1 from orange solid.

Daisy band
Make 1 from mutlicolored stripe.

Small tulip leaf
Make 1 from green print.

Large tulip leaf
Make 1 from green print.

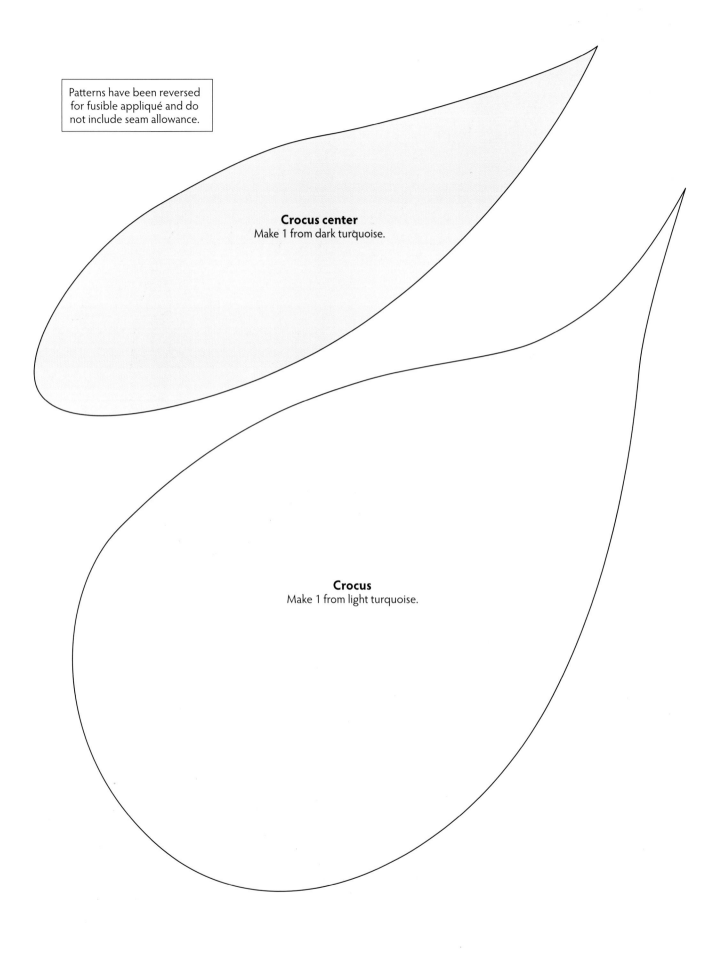

Patterns have been reversed for fusible appliqué and do not include seam allowance.

Crocus center
Make 1 from dark turquoise.

Crocus
Make 1 from light turquoise.

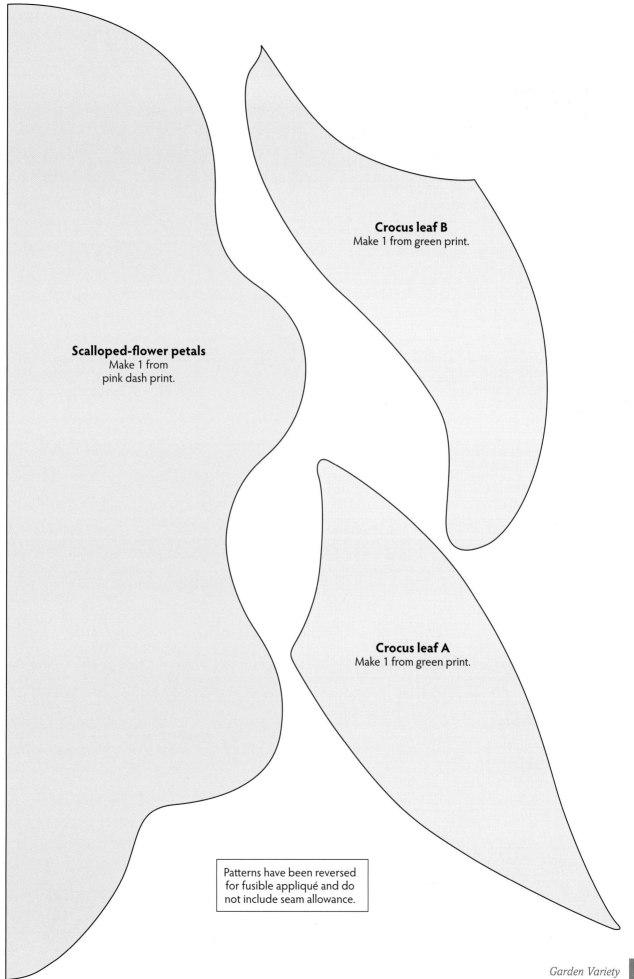

Crocus leaf B
Make 1 from green print.

Scalloped-flower petals
Make 1 from
pink dash print.

Crocus leaf A
Make 1 from green print.

Patterns have been reversed
for fusible appliqué and do
not include seam allowance.

"A Banner Day," designed by Jocelyn Ueng of It's Sew Emma;
pieced by Kimberly Jolly; quilted by Natalia Bonner

> Simple strips of bold prints are punctuated with a banner of festive flags. Choose the flag color wisely, and punch it up with a quilted accent!
>
> ~Jocelyn

MATERIALS

Yardage is based on 42"-wide fabric. Fat eighths are approximately 9" x 21".

1 fat eighth *each* of 6 assorted nondirectional prints* for pieced background

⅛ yard of cream solid for flags

⅓ yard of teal print for binding

⅔ yard of fabric for backing

21" x 25" piece of batting

Template plastic

*If you choose directional prints, you'll need 1 fat quarter (approximately 18" x 21") for each.

CUTTING

To make the flag pieces, trace patterns A–C on page 26 onto template plastic and cut them out. Lay the templates on the wrong side of the fabrics indicated and trace around them. Cut out the pieces on the traced lines. If you're using a directional print for any of the background strips, make sure you cut the pieces so they'll read correctly in the finished quilt.

From the cream solid, cut:

6 A triangles

From *each* of the 6 assorted-print fat eighths, cut:

1 rectangle, 3½" x 16½" (6 total)

1 square, 3½" x 3½" (6 total)

1 B triangle (6 total)

1 C triangle (6 total)

From the teal print, cut:

3 strips, 2" x 42"

ASSEMBLING THE QUILT TOP

1. Sew matching B and C triangles to opposite sides of a cream A triangle to make a flag unit. Press the seam allowances toward the B and C triangles. Repeat to make a total of six flag units. Square up each unit to measure 3½" x 3½".

Make 6.

2. Join a print 3½" square, the matching unit from step 1, and the matching print 3½" x 16½" rectangle as shown to make a vertical row. Press the seam allowances away from the units from step 1. Repeat to make a total of six rows.

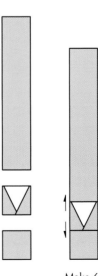

Make 6.

3. Arrange the rows side by side in an order that's pleasing to you. Sew the rows together along the long edges. Press the seam allowances in one direction.

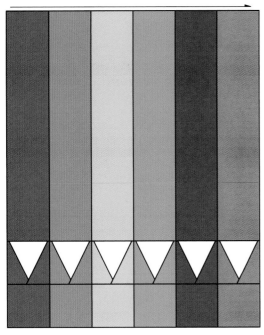

Quilt assembly

FINISHING THE QUILT

For help with any of the finishing techniques, go to ShopMartingale.com/HowtoQuilt to download free how-to information.

1. Layer the quilt top with backing and batting; baste the layers together.

2. Quilt as desired.

3. Bind the quilt edges using the teal 2"-wide strips.

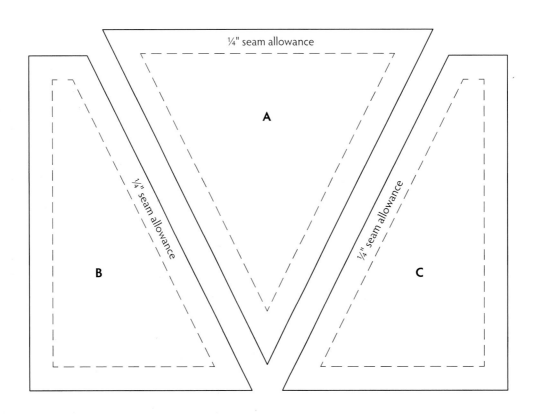

Hedgehog Heyday

FINISHED QUILT: 17½" x 22½" | FINISHED BLOCK: 8" x 8"

The sun is shining, the flowers are blooming . . . sounds like a heyday for hedgehogs! I used needle-turn appliqué to make the happy critters in the sample quilt come to life, but you could easily use whatever method you're comfortable with.

~Cheri

MATERIALS

Yardage is based on 42"-wide fabric. Fat quarters are approximately 18" x 21".

½ yard of white tone on tone for blocks and border

⅜ yard of blue print for blocks and binding

1 fat quarter of green print for stem and leaf appliqués

1 fat quarter of brown print for hedgehog body appliqués

⅛ yard of coral print for blocks

⅛ yard of green print for blocks

⅛ yard of tan print for hedgehog face and leg appliqués and butterfly bodies

⅛ yard of coral solid for flower appliqués

Scrap of light-yellow print for flower center and butterfly wing appliqués

Scrap of yellow print for butterfly wing appliqués

⅔ yard of fabric for backing

20" x 25" piece of batting

Black and coral 6-strand embroidery floss

Size 9 embroidery needle

Scrap of template plastic

CUTTING

From the white tone on tone, cut:
1 strip, 4" x 42"; crosscut into 2 rectangles, 4" x 18"
1 strip, 8" x 42"; crosscut into 4 squares, 8" x 8"

From the blue print, cut:
2 strips, 2⅜" x 42"
3 strips, 2¼" x 42"

From *each* of the coral and green prints for blocks, cut:
1 strip, 2⅜" x 42" (2 total)

MAKING THE APPLIQUÉD PIECES

1. Using the patterns on pages 31–33 and referring to the photo on page 28 for fabric choices, prepare the appliqué pieces for four hedgehogs, two butterflies, five large leaves, and 28 small leaves, as well as approximately 50" of ¼"-wide finished bias-cut stems. Because the patterns were intended for needle-turn appliqué, be aware that the patterns will produce shapes that reflect the same orientation as those on the quilt shown. For other methods, such as fusible-web appliqué, you may need to reverse the patterns.

2. Fold each white 8" square in half diagonally in both directions. Finger-press the folds to mark the centers. Working in numerical order, appliqué the prepared pieces for each block onto a square, aligning the pattern center with the square center, and keeping in mind that the blocks are appliquéd on point and that the flowers will be added later.

3. Using two strands of black floss and the embroidery needle, satin stitch the eyes and noses of each hedgehog. Outline the eyes and make the eyelashes using a stem stitch. Stem-stitch the mouths. Using one strand of black floss, stem-stitch the outline of

"Hedgehog Heyday," designed and made by Cheri Leffler

the face, the mouth, the antennae, and the legs of each butterfly. Work a colonial knot at the end of each antennae and for each eye.

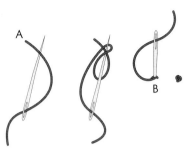

Colonial knot

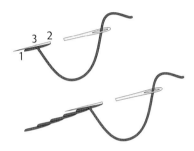

Stem stitch

Satin stitch

4. Press each appliquéd square and then trim to 6½" x 6½", keeping the designs centered.

5. Fold each white rectangle in half vertically and horizontally. Finger-press the folds to mark the center. Cut two 13" lengths of the ¼"-wide bias stem prepared in step 1 on page 27. Center a green bias strip on the horizontal crease line of each rectangle and appliqué it in place. Working in numerical order,

appliqué the small leaves in place on each rectangle. The flowers will be added later.

6. Press each appliquéd rectangle and then trim to 3" x 17½", keeping the designs centered.

MAKING THE BLOCKS

1. Stitch the blue, green, and coral 2⅜" x 42" strips together along the long edges as shown to make a strip set. Press the seam allowances as indicated. Crosscut the strip set into four segments, 7¼" wide. Square up each segment to 7¼" x 7¼", keeping the seam between the green and coral strips centered.

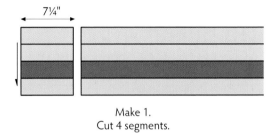

Make 1.
Cut 4 segments.

2. Cut each segment from step 1 into quarters diagonally to make four triangles (16 total).

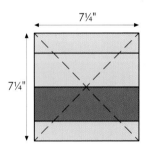

3. Lay out the appliquéd squares on point, referring to the photo (page 28) as needed. Arrange the triangles from step 2 around the appliquéd squares as shown, with the triangles forming a coral pinwheel in the center of the quilt top. Join the triangles on opposite sides of each square first, and then add the remaining two triangles to each square. Press the seam allowances toward the triangles. Because

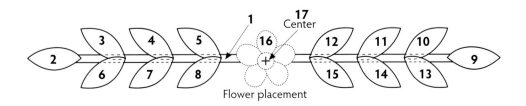

Border appliqué placement

the bias edges of the triangles are on the outside of the block, you may wish to stay stitch 1/8" from the edges of each block to prevent them from stretching.

4. Trace the flower-petal pattern on page 31 onto template plastic and cut it out.

5. Using the template, trace 35 petal shapes onto the coral solid fabric right side. Cut out each petal, adding 1/4" for seam allowance. Finger press the seam allowances of the curved edges under on each petal shape.

6. Thread a hand-sewing needle with all-purpose thread and knot one end. Baste along the bottom edge of five petals, stitching one right after another without cutting the thread.

7. Pull the thread end to gather the petals, and then bring the two end petals together to form a circle. Secure the first petal to the last petal to maintain the flower shape. Repeat with the remaining petals to make a total of seven flower units.

8. Place a completed flower unit where indicated on each block and each appliquéd rectangle. Hand appliqué each flower unit in place. Appliqué a center circle to the middle of each flower.

ASSEMBLING THE QUILT TOP

1. Arrange the hedgehog blocks in two horizontal rows of two blocks each as shown. Sew the blocks in each row together. Press the seam allowance open. Sew the rows together. Press the seam allowances open.

2. Join the appliquéd rectangles to the top and bottom edges of the quilt top. Press the seam allowances toward the rectangles.

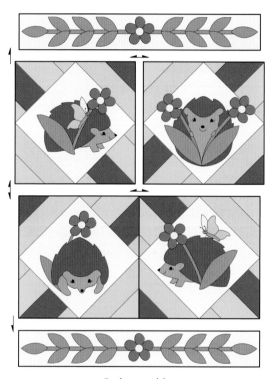

Quilt assembly

FINISHING THE QUILT

For help with any of the finishing techniques, go to ShopMartingale.com/HowtoQuilt to download free how-to information.

1. Layer the quilt top with backing and batting; baste the layers together.

2. Quilt as desired.

3. Bind the quilt edges using the blue 2 1/4"-wide strips.

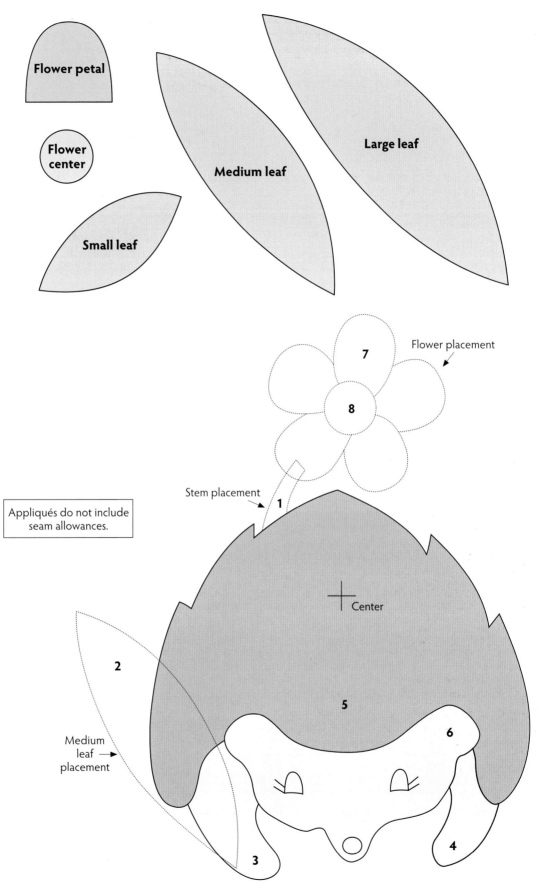

Flower petal

Flower center

Small leaf

Medium leaf

Large leaf

Flower placement

7

8

Stem placement

1

Appliqués do not include seam allowances.

Center

2

5

6

Medium leaf placement

3

4

Lower-left block

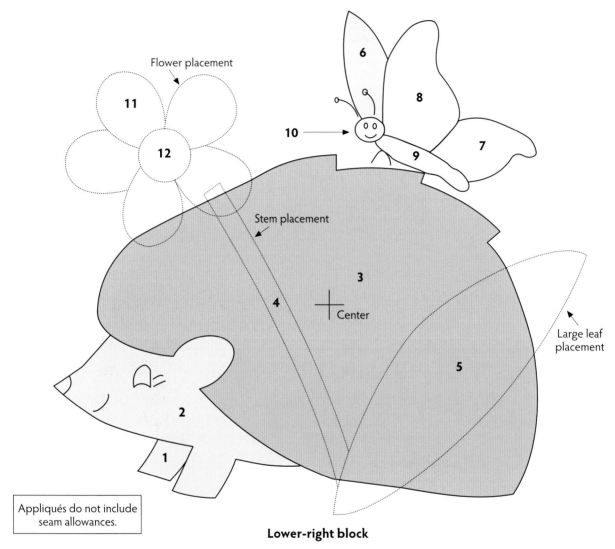

Flower placement

11

12

Stem placement

6

8

10

9

7

3

4

Center

5

Large leaf
placement

2

1

Appliqués do not include
seam allowances.

Lower-right block

Reverse pattern for upper-left block, placing butterfly on stem.

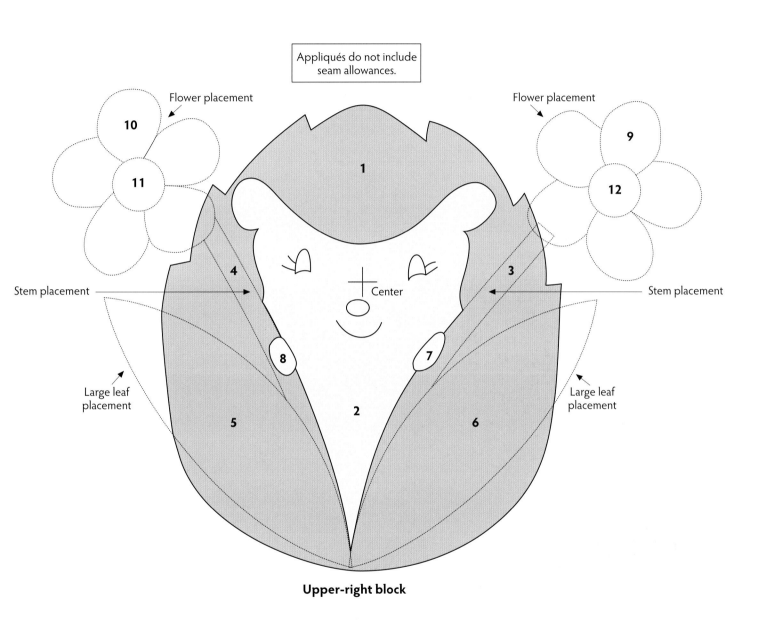

Appliqués do not include seam allowances.

Flower placement

10

11

Flower placement

9

12

Stem placement

Stem placement

Center

4

3

Large leaf placement

Large leaf placement

8

7

5

2

6

Upper-right block

"Fox in a Box," designed and made by Jeni Baker

Fox in a Box

FINISHED QUILT: 18½" x 18½" | FINISHED BLOCK: 6" x 6"

A sweet and simple block reveals hidden foxes when turned on point—so adorable, you'll want to make an entire den of fox blocks from your favorite fabrics.

~Jeni

MATERIALS

Yardage is based on 42"-wide fabric.

2½" x 12" strip *each* of 9 assorted prints for blocks

1½" x 15" strip of black solid for blocks

⅔ yard of white solid for background and binding

⅔ yard of fabric for backing

21" x 21" piece of batting

18 black buttons, ½" diameter, for eyes

CUTTING

From *each* of the 9 print strips, cut:

2 squares, 2½" x 2½" (18 total)

3 squares, 2" x 2" (27 total)

From the black solid, cut:

9 squares, 1½" x 1½"

From the white solid, cut:

2 strips, 2" x 42"; crosscut into:

    9 rectangles, 2" x 3½"

    9 squares, 2" x 2"

3 strips, 2½" x 42"; crosscut *1 of the strips* into

    16 squares, 2½" x 2½"

2 strips, 4" x 42"; crosscut into 18 squares, 4" x 4"; cut

    in half diagonally to make 36 triangles

2 squares, 2½" x 2½"

MAKING THE BLOCKS

1. Draw a diagonal line from corner to corner on the wrong side of each white 2½" square. Place a marked square on a print 2½" square, right sides together. Stitch ¼" from both sides of the marked line. Cut the squares apart on the marked line to make two half-square-triangle units. Press the seam allowances open. Repeat with the remaining marked white squares and print 2½" squares to make a total of 36 units. Trim each half-square-triangle unit to measure 2" x 2".

Make 36.

2. Select one 2" square from each of the nine prints. Draw a diagonal line from corner to corner on the wrong side of each black 1½" square. Place a marked square on one corner of a print 2" square as shown. Sew on the marked line. Trim ¼" from the stitching line. Press the seam allowances toward the corner. Repeat with the remaining marked black squares and the eight print 2" squares to make a total of nine nose units.

Make 9.

3. Using pieces with the same print, arrange three half-square-triangle units from step 1, one nose unit from step 2, two print 2" squares, one white 2" square, and one white 2" x 3½" rectangle in three horizontal rows as shown. Sew the pieces in each row together. Press the seam allowances open. Sew the rows together. Press the seam allowances open. Repeat to make a total of nine units. You will have one half-square-triangle unit from each print left over.

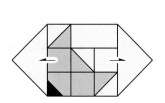

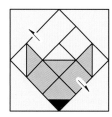

Make 9.

4. Center and sew white triangles to opposite sides of each unit from step 3. Press the seam allowances toward the triangles. Repeat on the remaining two sides. Trim each block to 6½" x 6½".

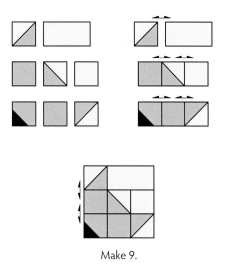

Make 9.

ASSEMBLING THE QUILT TOP

Arrange the blocks in three horizontal rows of three blocks each. Sew the blocks in each row together. Press the seam allowances in opposite directions from row to row. Sew the rows together. Press the seam allowances in one direction.

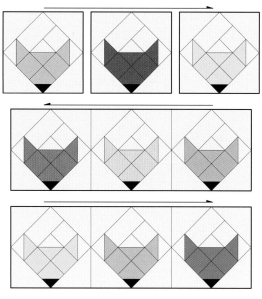

Quilt assembly

FINISHING THE QUILT

For help with any of the finishing techniques, go to ShopMartingale.com/HowtoQuilt to download free how-to information.

1. Layer the quilt top with backing and batting; baste the layers together.

2. Quilt as desired.

3. Bind the quilt edges using the white 2½"-wide strips.

4. Sew a button to the center of each print square within the blocks for the fox eyes.

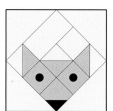

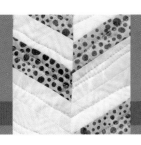

Tapa Cloth

FINISHED QUILT: 18½" x 21½"

I n the Pacific islands, the giving of tapa cloth, originally made by pounding bark from specific trees into cloth and then decorating it with various geometric designs, was considered a very special gesture. This fat-quarter quilt is a small geometric representation of traditional tapa cloth. Offer this modern version as your gift to a special someone.

~Natalie

MATERIALS

Yardage is based on 42"-wide fabric. Fat quarters are approximately 18" x 21".

5 fat quarters of assorted orange batiks for pieced-square rows and binding

3 fat quarters of assorted blue-gray batiks for chevron panels (2 light prints and 1 dark print in the quilt shown)

⅔ yard of fabric for backing

21" x 24" piece of batting

CUTTING

From the blue-gray batiks, cut a *total* of:

7 strips, 2⅜" x 21"; crosscut into 20 rectangles, 2⅜" x 7"

10 strips, 2¼" x 21"; crosscut into 38 rectangles, 2¼" x 5"

3 strips, 1⅜" x 21"; crosscut into 12 rectangles, 1⅜" x 5"

3 strips, 1½" x 21"; crosscut into 8 rectangles, 1½" x 7"

From 1 of the orange batiks, cut:

5 strips, 2" x 21"

2 strips, 1½" x 10½"

From the remaining 4 orange batiks, cut a *total* of:

14 strips, 1½" x 10½"

4 squares, 1½" x 1½"

"Tapa Cloth," designed and made by Natalie Barnes; fabrics by Hoffman California Fabrics

MAKING THE CHEVRON PANELS

1. To make the wide center panel, lay out the 20 blue-gray 2⅜" x 7" rectangles and the eight blue-gray 1½" x 7" rectangles into two side-by-side rows, using half the pieces of each size in each row and beginning and ending the rows with the wider rectangles. In the sample quilt, the rectangle widths in each row followed the same sequence, but you can rearrange as needed to create the desired look. When you're pleased with the arrangement, stack the strips from top to bottom for the left and right sides of the panel.

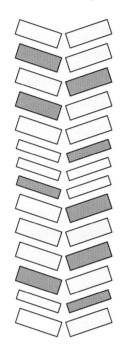

2. With a gridded cutting mat by your sewing machine, place the top left rectangle on the cutting board with the bottom edge centered diagonally on a 1 x 3 grid as shown.

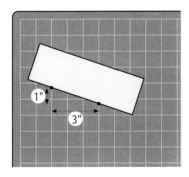

3. Working with the left column only, place the next rectangle on top of the first rectangle, right sides together, staggering the left end ½". Sew the rectangles together along their lower edges. Press the seam allowances toward the newly added rectangle. Continue adding rectangles in this manner until all of the rectangles in the stack have been added.

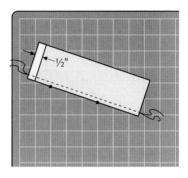

4. Repeat steps 2 and 3 with the stack of rectangles for the right side of the chevron panel, pressing all of the seam allowances toward the top rectangle.

5. Lay the left column on your cutting mat at the same angle you used in step 2. Trim both staggered edges so they are straight and the panel measures 3½" wide. Repeat with the right-side column.

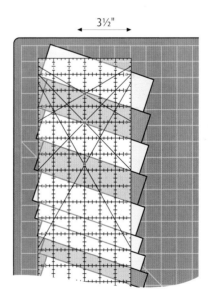

6. Pin and sew the left and right columns together, carefully matching seam intersections. Press the seam allowances open.

7. Trim the top and bottom of the panel ¼" from the first seam on each end.

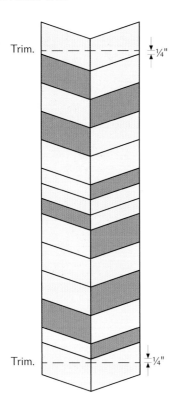

Trim. ↕¼"

Trim. ↕¼"

8. To make the narrow side chevron panels, refer to step 1 to select and lay out 16 blue-gray 2¼" x 5" rectangles and eight blue-gray 1⅜" x 5" rectangles for the left panel and 22 blue-gray 2¼" x 5" rectangles and four blue-gray 1⅜" x 5" rectangles for the right panel. Repeat steps 2–7 to assemble the narrow chevron panels in the same manner as for the wide panel, but center the first rectangle in the stack on a 1 x 2 grid and stagger the ends ¾" when you sew them together. Trim the rows to 2½" wide and then sew them together and trim the ends straight.

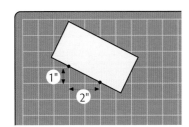

1"
2"

MAKING THE PIECED-SQUARES ROWS AND RECTANGLE

1. Randomly select four assorted orange batik 1½" x 10½" strips and sew them together along the long edges to make a strip set. Press the seam allowances in one direction. Repeat to make a total of four strip sets. Crosscut the strip sets into 24 segments, 1½" wide.

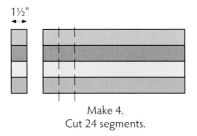

1½"

Make 4.
Cut 24 segments.

2. Randomly select five segments from step 1. Arrange the segments in five vertical columns, alternating the direction of the seam allowances so they'll nest together when joined. Sew the segments together. Press the seam allowances in one direction.

Make 1.

3. Randomly select four segments from step 1 and sew them together end to end to make a pieced-squares column. Add an assorted orange 1½" square to the end of the strip. Press the seam allowances in one direction.

4. Randomly select five segments from step 1 and sew them together end to end. Add an orange 1½" square to the end of the strip. Press the seam allowances in one direction. Repeat to make a total of three strips. Sew the strips together along the long edges. Press the seam allowances in one direction.

ASSEMBLING THE QUILT TOP

1. Refer to the quilt assembly diagram to arrange the chevron panels and pieced-squares rows and rectangle as shown.

2. Sew the narrow orange column to the right edge of the left chevron panel. Press the seam allowances open. Sew the pieced rectangle to the bottom of this unit. Press the seam allowances open.

3. Join the rows. Press the seam allowances open.

FINISHING THE QUILT

For help with any of the finishing techniques, go to ShopMartingale.com/HowtoQuilt to download free how-to information.

1. Layer the quilt top with backing and batting; baste the layers together.

2. Quilt as desired.

3. Bind quilt edges using the orange 2"-wide strips.

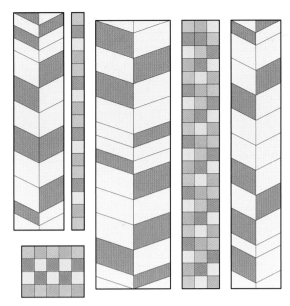

Quilt assembly

Alternate Colorway

In this variation of "Tapa Cloth," Natalie replaced the cotton batiks with subtle linen fabrics. They're more loosely woven, allowing Natalie to add chunky hand-quilting details.

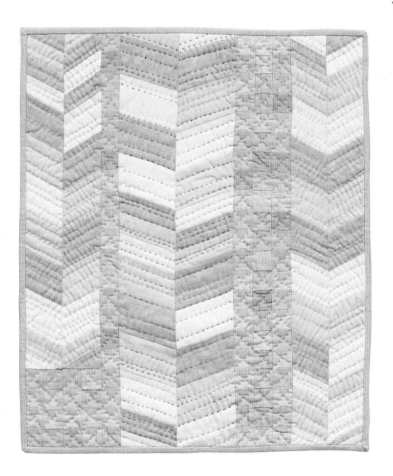

"White Stars," designed and pieced by Julie Herman; quilted by Angela Walters

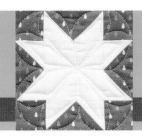

White Stars

Against an assortment of bright and dark fabrics for the background, the solid white stars really shine. Play with the negative space during the quilting process to make it absolutely stellar!

~Julie

MATERIALS

Yardage is based on 42"-wide fabric. Fat quarters are approximately 18" x 21".

5" x 7" rectangle *each* of 12 assorted prints for blocks

⅓ yard of white solid for blocks

⅛ yard of red-and-white print for single-fold binding

1 fat quarter of fabric for backing

16" x 20" piece of batting

CUTTING

From *each* of the 12 assorted prints, cut:
4 rectangles, 1½" x 2½" (48 total)
4 squares, 1½" x 1½" (48 total)

From the white solid, cut:
1 strip, 2½" x 42"; crosscut into 12 squares, 2½" x 2½"
4 strips, 1½" x 42"; crosscut into 96 squares, 1½" x 1½"

From the pink-and-white print, cut:
2 strips, 1¼" x 42"*

For double-fold binding, cut 2 strips 2" x 42".

MAKING THE BLOCKS

1. Draw a diagonal line from corner to corner on the wrong side of each white 1½" square. Place a marked square on one end of an assorted-print rectangle, right sides together. Sew on the marked line. Trim ¼" from the stitching line. Press the seam allowances open. Repeat on the opposite end of the rectangle, orienting the marked line as shown. Repeat with the remaining marked squares and assorted-print rectangles to make a total of 48 flying-geese units.

Make 48.

2. Arrange four matching flying-geese units, four matching print 1½" squares, and a white 2½" square into three horizontal rows as shown. Sew the pieces in each row together. Press the seam allowances open. Sew the rows together. Press the seam allowances open. Repeat to make a total of 12 blocks.

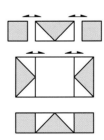 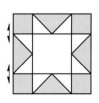

Make 12.

ASSEMBLING THE QUILT TOP

Refer to the quilt assembly diagram to arrange the blocks into four rows of three blocks each. Sew the blocks in each row together. Press the seam allowances open. Sew the rows together. Press the seam allowances open.

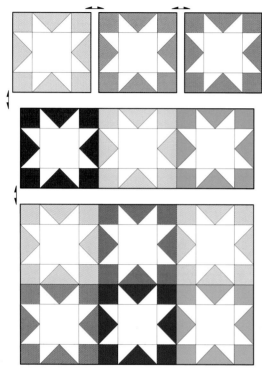

Quilt assembly

FINISHING THE QUILT

For help with any of the finishing techniques, go to ShopMartingale.com/HowtoQuilt to download free how-to information.

1. Layer the quilt top with backing and batting; baste the layers together.

2. Quilt as desired.

3. Sew the pink-and-white 1¼"-wide strips together at right angles to make one long strip. Press the seam allowances open. Press under one long raw edge ¼".

4. With the raw edges aligned, stitch the binding strip to the quilt edges in the same manner as you would for double-fold binding, mitering the corners. Fold the binding to the quilt back and stitch the folded edge in place.

Sunshine

FINISHED QUILT: 18" x 18" | FINISHED BLOCK: 3½" x 3½"

Petite pinwheels are quite charming. Put an unexpected spin on a two-color quilt by adding a contrasting colored block for a small but certain impact.

~Kimberly

MATERIALS

Yardage is based on 42"-wide fabric.

½ yard of white solid for blocks, sashing, and border

⅜ yard of yellow print for blocks

¼ yard of gray print #1 for sashing squares and binding

⅛ yard of gray print #2 for block

⅝ yard of fabric for backing

20" x 20" piece of batting

CUTTING

From the white solid, cut:

4 strips, 1⅜" x 42"; crosscut into 64 rectangles, 1⅜" x 2¼"

2 strips, 1½" x 42"; crosscut into:
    2 strips, 1½" x 16"
    2 strips, 1½" x 18"

3 strips, 1" x 42"; crosscut into 24 rectangles, 1" x 4"

From the yellow print, cut:

8 strips, 1⅜" x 42"; crosscut into:
    60 rectangles, 1⅜" x 2¼"
    120 squares, 1⅜" x 1⅜"

From gray print #2, cut:

1 strip, 1⅜" x 42"; crosscut into:
    4 rectangles, 1⅜" x 2¼"
    8 squares, 1⅜" x 1⅜"

From gray print #1, cut:

9 squares, 1" x 1"*

3 strips, 2" x 42"

Kimberly fussy cut her gray squares to feature a starburst design in each one.

MAKING THE BLOCKS

1. Draw a diagonal line from corner to corner on the wrong side of each yellow 1⅜" square. Place a marked square on one end of a white 1⅜" x 2¼" rectangle, right sides together. Sew on the marked line. Trim ¼" from the stitching line. Press the seam allowances toward the yellow. Repeat on the opposite end of the rectangle, orienting the marked line as shown. Repeat to sew the remaining yellow marked squares to white rectangles for a total of 60 flying-geese units.

Make 60.

2. Sew a yellow 1⅜" x 2¼" rectangle to each flying-geese unit as shown. Press the seam allowances toward the rectangles.

Make 60.

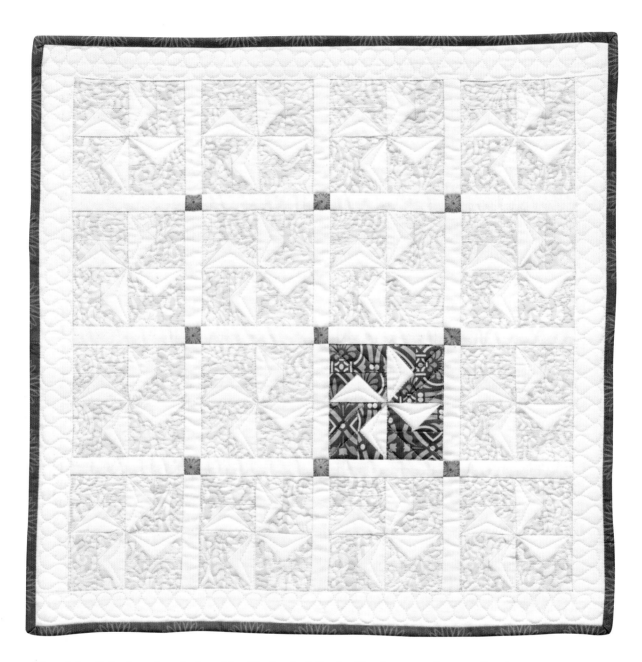

"Sunshine," designed and pieced by Kimberly Jolly for Fat Quarter Shop; quilted by Natalia Bonner

3. Arrange four units from step 2 into two horizontal rows of two units each. Sew the units in each row together. Press the seam allowances in opposite directions. Sew the rows together. Press the seam allowances in either direction. Repeat to make a total of 15 blocks.

Make 15.

4. Repeat steps 1–3 with the gray print #2 squares and rectangles and the four remaining white 1⅜" x 2¼" rectangles to make one block.

Make 1.

ASSEMBLING THE QUILT TOP

1. Alternately arrange four yellow blocks and three white 1" x 4" sashing rectangles into a block row. Sew the pieces together. Press the seam allowances toward the sashing rectangles. Repeat to make a total of three block rows.

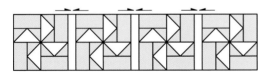

Make 3.

2. Alternately arrange three yellow blocks and the single gray block with three white 1" x 4" sashing rectangles into a block row as shown. Sew the pieces together. Press the seam allowances toward the sashing rectangles.

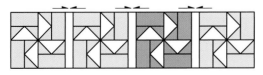

Make 1.

3. Alternately arrange four white 1" x 4" sashing rectangles and three gray print #1 sashing squares into a sashing row. Sew the pieces together. Press the seam allowances toward the sashing rectangles. Repeat to make a total of three rows.

Make 3.

4. Refer to the quilt assembly diagram to alternately arrange the block rows and sashing rows. Sew the rows together. Press the seam allowances toward the sashing rows.

5. Sew the white 1½" x 16" border strips to the sides of the quilt top. Press the seam allowances toward the border strips. Sew the white 1½" x 18" border strips to the top and bottom of the quilt top. Press the seam allowances toward the border strips.

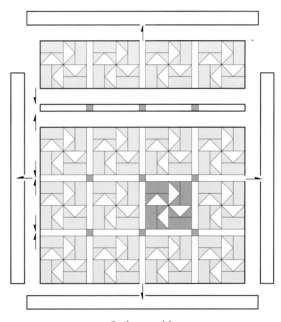

Quilt assembly

FINISHING THE QUILT

For help with any of the finishing techniques, go to ShopMartingale.com/HowtoQuilt to download free how-to information.

1. Layer the quilt top with backing and batting; baste the layers together.

2. Quilt as desired.

3. Bind the quilt edges using the 2"-wide gray print #1 strips.

"My Little Garden," designed and made by Jackie White

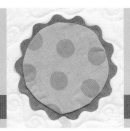

My Little Garden

FINISHED QUILT: 22" x 17"

This whimsical little piece captures the essence of spring in bloom. Using rickrack for stems and buttons for flower centers makes it extra special and dimensional.

~Jackie

MATERIALS

Yardage is based on 42"-wide fabric. Fat quarters are approximately 18" x 21".

⅓ yard of light-blue print for sky

¼ yard of gray stripe for fence

¼ yard of gray print for ground

5" x 10" rectangle *each* of blue, orange, dark-pink, yellow, and red medium-scale polka-dot prints for flower appliqués

4" x 12" rectangle *each* of 5 assorted small-scale polka-dot prints for leaf appliqués

4" x 4" square *each* of 2 assorted polka-dot prints for bird appliqués

1 fat quarter of green polka-dot print for binding

⅝ yard of fabric for backing

26" x 26" square of batting

1⅓ yards of green medium rickrack for stems

½ yard *each* of blue, orange, and red medium rickrack for flowers

5" x 5" square of paper-backed fusible web

2 or 3 buttons, ½" to ¾" diameter, for flower embellishments

Black 6-strand embroidery floss for birds' eyes and legs

Size 9 embroidery needle

Template plastic

CUTTING

From the light-blue print, cut:
1 rectangle, 9" x 22"

From the gray stripe, cut:
1 strip, 4" x 22"

From the gray print, cut:
1 strip, 5½" x 22"

From the batting, cut:
1 rectangle, 19" x 24"
5 squares, 4" x 4"

From the green polka-dot print, cut:
5 strips, 2½" x 21"

MAKING THE BACKGROUND

Join the light-blue, gray-striped, and gray-print rectangles along the long edges as shown to make the appliqué background. Press the seam allowances toward the gray stripe.

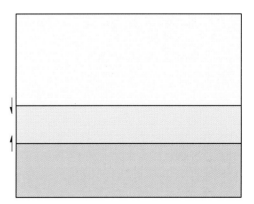

MAKING THE APPLIQUÉS

1. Trace the flower circle, batting circle, and leaf patterns on page 51 onto template plastic and cut out.

2. Using the batting circle template, trace and cut out a circle from each 4" batting square.

3. To make the plain flowers, fold the red and yellow polka-dot 5" x 10" rectangles in half right sides together to make 5" squares. Using the flower circle template, trace a circle onto each folded piece. Stitch on the marked line of each piece, backstitching at the beginning and end. Cut out each circle ¼" from the stitching line. Make a slit approximately 1" long in the center of one circle of each piece, being careful not to cut through both layers. Turn the circles to the right side through the slit and use a blunt tool to smooth out the seam. Insert a batting circle through the slit of each piece and smooth it out; press.

4. To make the rickrack flowers, fold the blue, orange, and pink polka-dot 5" x 10" rectangles in half right sides together to make 5" squares. Using the flower circle template, trace a circle onto one side of each piece. Cut out the circles on the marked lines. Lay a coordinating piece of rickrack on the right side of one circle of each color so that the rickrack edge just touches the edge of the circle; overlap the ends just beyond the edge of each circle. Baste the rickrack in place, easing the trim around the circles as you stitch.

5. Lay the matching circle over each circle from step 4. Stitch ¼" from the edges. Trim the rickrack ends that extend beyond the circles. Refer to step 3 to make a slit in one of the circles of each pair, turn the circles to the right side, and insert a batting circle.

6. To make the leaves, fold each polka-dot 4" x 12" rectangle in half right sides together to make a 4" x 6" piece. Using the leaf template, trace two leaves onto each of three of the folded pieces; trace three leaf shapes onto the remaining two rectangles. Stitch on the marked lines, backstitching at the beginning and end. Cut out each leaf ⅛" from the stitching lines. Make a slit approximately ¾" long in the center of each leaf piece, being careful not to cut through both layers. Turn the leaves to the right side through the slit and use a blunt tool to smooth out the seam.

7. To make the birds, use the pattern on page 51 to trace one bird and one reversed bird onto the paper side of the fusible-web square. Roughly cut out the bird shapes. Fuse a shape to the wrong side of each polka-dot 4" square. Cut out the pieces on the marked lines. Remove the paper backing.

ASSEMBLING THE QUILT TOP

1. Cut the green rickrack into one piece each of the following lengths: 13", 12", 9", 8", and 6".

2. Referring to the diagram below and the photo (page 48) as needed, arrange the stems and flowers on the background. When you're happy with the placement, remove the flowers and stitch through the center of the rickrack stems to secure them. Replace the flowers and hand appliqué them in place.

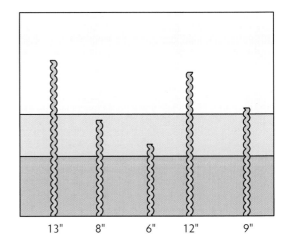

3. Position the birds on the background where desired, leaving enough room below them to embroider the legs; fuse them into place. Using two strands of black floss, backstitch the legs and make a French knot for each eye.

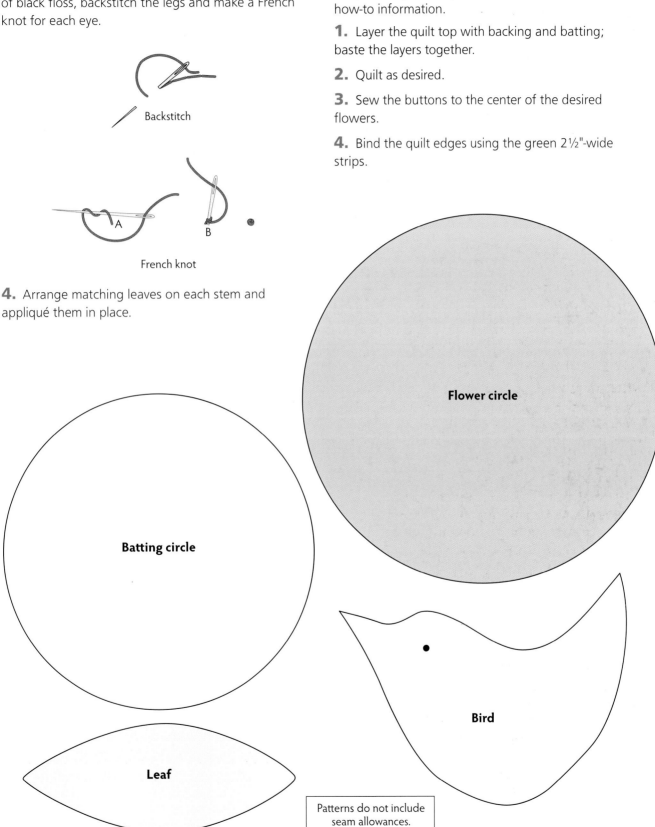

Backstitch

French knot

4. Arrange matching leaves on each stem and appliqué them in place.

FINISHING THE QUILT

For help with any of the finishing techniques, go to ShopMartingale.com/HowtoQuilt to download free how-to information.

1. Layer the quilt top with backing and batting; baste the layers together.

2. Quilt as desired.

3. Sew the buttons to the center of the desired flowers.

4. Bind the quilt edges using the green 2½"-wide strips.

Flower circle

Batting circle

Bird

Leaf

Patterns do not include seam allowances.

"HI!," designed and pieced by Kimberly Jolly for Fat Quarter Shop; quilted by Natalia Bonner

> This is the friendliest little quilt you'll ever meet! One block says it all and couldn't be easier to piece.
>
> ~Kimberly

MATERIALS

Yardage is based on 42"-wide fabric. Fat eighths are approximately 9" x 21".

1 fat eighth *each* of blue print #1, yellow print #1, gray print #1, gray print #2, and cream print for blocks

⅜ yard of yellow print #2 for blocks and binding

⅓ yard of white solid for blocks and border

¼ yard of blue print #2 for blocks

⅔ yard of fabric for backing

20" x 20" piece of batting

CUTTING

From the white solid, cut:

4 strips, 1¾" x 42"; crosscut into:

    2 strips, 1¾" x 18"

    2 strips, 1¾" x 15½"

    32 squares, 1¾" x 1¾"

From blue print #2, cut:

2 strips, 1¾" x 42"; crosscut into:

    8 rectangles, 1¾" x 4¼"

    4 squares, 1¾" x 1¾"

From blue print #1, cut:

3 strips, 1¾" x 21"; crosscut into:

    6 rectangles, 1¾" x 4¼"

    3 squares, 1¾" x 1¾"

From yellow print #2, cut:

1 strip, 1¾" x 42"; crosscut into:

    6 rectangles, 1¾" x 4¼"

    3 squares, 1¾" x 1¾"

3 strips, 2" x 42"

From *each* of yellow print #1 and gray print #1, cut:

2 strips, 1¾" x 21"; crosscut into:

    4 rectangles, 1¾" x 4¼" (8 total)

    2 squares, 1¾" x 1¾" (4 total)

From *each* of gray print #2 and the cream print, cut:

1 strip, 1¾" x 21"; crosscut into:

    2 rectangles, 1¾" x 4¼" (4 total)

    1 square, 1¾" x 1¾" (2 total)

MAKING THE BLOCKS

1. Sew white squares to opposite sides of each 1¾" print square to make a total of 16 units. Press the seam allowances toward the print squares.

Blue print #2.
Make 4.

Gray print #1.
Make 2.

Blue print #1.
Make 3.

Gray print #2.
Make 1.

Yellow print #2.
Make 3.

Cream print.
Make 1.

Yellow print #1.
Make 2.

2. Sew matching print rectangles to opposite sides of each unit from step 1 as shown to make a total of 16 blocks. Press the seam allowances toward the rectangles.

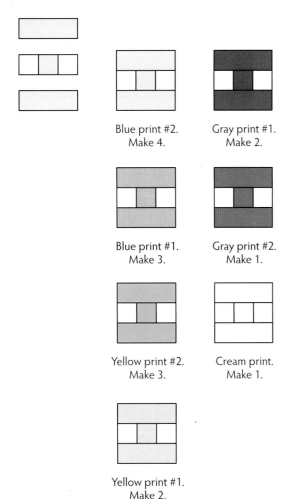

Blue print #2.
Make 4.

Gray print #1.
Make 2.

Blue print #1.
Make 3.

Gray print #2.
Make 1.

Yellow print #2.
Make 3.

Cream print.
Make 1.

Yellow print #1.
Make 2.

ASSEMBLING THE QUILT TOP

1. Refer to the quilt assembly diagram to arrange the blocks into four rows of four blocks each, with the prints positioned so they run diagonally across the quilt. Sew the blocks in each row together. Press the seam allowances in opposite directions from row to row. Sew the rows together. Press the seam allowances in one direction.

2. Sew the white 1¾" x 15½" border strips to the sides of the quilt top. Press the seam allowances toward the border strips. Sew the white 1¾" x 18" border strips to the top and bottom of the quilt top. Press the seam allowances toward the border strips.

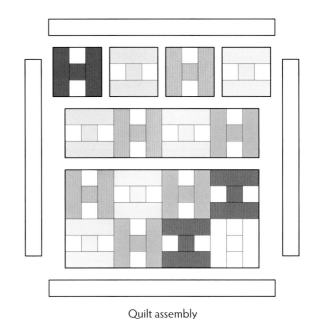

Quilt assembly

FINISHING THE QUILT

For help with any of the finishing techniques, go to ShopMartingale.com/HowtoQuilt to download free how-to information.

1. Layer the quilt top with backing and batting; baste the layers together.

2. Quilt as desired.

3. Bind the quilt edges using the 2"-wide yellow print #2 strips.

Starlight

Foundation paper piecing is a great way to achieve crisp, sharp angles and corners in your quilt blocks. This mini-quilt features three different paper-pieced stars, surrounded by lots of negative space to put extra emphasis on the blocks.

~Elizabeth

MATERIALS

Yardage is based on 42"-wide fabric. Fat eighths are approximately 9" x 21".

½ yard of black print for sashing, inner border, and binding

⅓ yard of light-gray print for outer border

⅛ yard or 1 fat eighth *each* of yellow #1, yellow #2, gold #1, gold #2, light-aqua #1, light aqua #2, dark-aqua #1, dark-aqua #2, purple #1, purple #2, teal, fuchsia #1, fuchsia #2 for stars

8" x 11" rectangle of gray print #1 for block A background

10" x 11" rectangle of gray print #2 for block B background

9" x 9" square of gray print #3 for block C background

Scraps of assorted yellow and gold prints for block A corners

⅔ yard of fabric for backing

21" x 25" piece of batting

Copy or foundation-piecing paper

CUTTING

From gray print #1, cut:
8 rectangles, 2½" x 3½" (Block A, pieces A1 and B1)

From *each* of purple prints #1 and #2, cut:
4 rectangles, 1½" x 2½" (8 total; Block A, pieces A2 and B2)

From *each* of light-aqua print #1 and dark aqua print #1, cut:
4 squares, 2½" x 2½" (8 total; Block A, pieces A3 and B3)

From the assorted yellow scraps, cut:
4 squares, 2" x 2" (Block A, piece A4)

From the assorted gold scraps, cut:
4 squares, 2" x 2" (Block A, piece B4)

From gray print #2, cut:
8 rectangles, 2" x 4" (Block B, pieces A1 and B1)

From the teal print, cut:
8 rectangles, 1¾" x 4½" (Block B, pieces A2 and B2)

From *each* of yellow #1, gold #1, fuschia #1, and fuschia #2, cut:
2 rectangles, 2" x 4½" (8 total; Block B, pieces A3 and B3)

From yellow #2, cut:
4 rectangles, 1½" x 3½" (Block C, piece A2)
4 rectangles, 1½" x 2½" (Block C, piece C2)

From *each* of dark-aqua #1 and dark-aqua #2, cut:
4 squares, 2½" x 2½" (Block C, pieces A1 and D1)

From gray print #3, cut:
8 rectangles, 2" x 4" (Block C, pieces B1 and C1)

From gold #2, cut:
4 rectangles, 1½" x 3½" (Block C, piece D2)
4 squares, 1½" x 2½" (Block C, piece B2)

Continued on page 57.

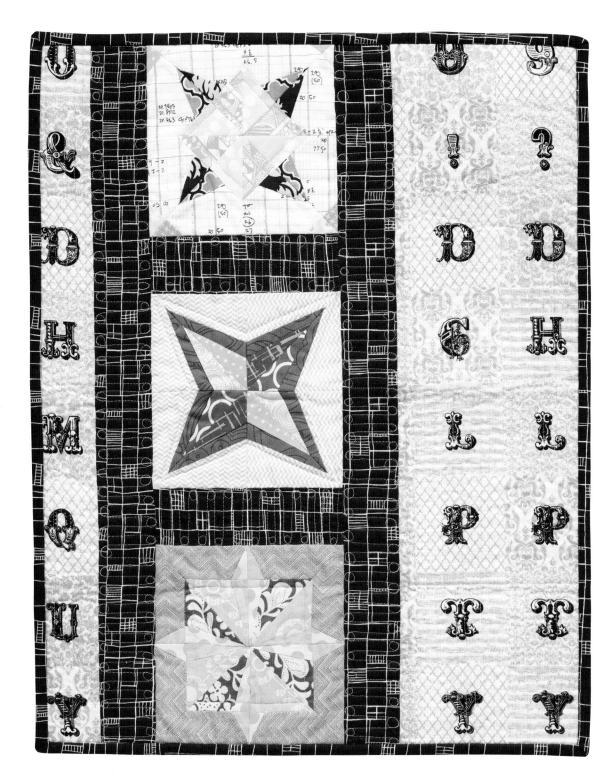

"Starlight," designed and made by Elizabeth Dackson

Continued from page 55.

From the black print, cut:
2 rectangles, 2¾" x 6½"
2 strips, 2¾" x 23"
3 strips, 2½" x 42"

From the light-gray print, cut:
1 strip, 2¾" x 23"
1 strip, 5¾" x 23"

PAPER PIECING THE BLOCKS

1. Using the patterns on pages 58 and 59, trace or photocopy each pattern onto copy or foundation-piecing paper four times.

2. Paper piece each section using the fabrics indicated on the pattern. For block B, paper piece two A3 sections with fuchsia #1 and two A3 sections with yellow #1. Paper piece two B3 sections with fuchsia #2 and two B3 sections with gold #1. Make four A and B sections for each block, as well as four C and D sections for block C. Trim along the outer lines of each unit.

3. For blocks A and B, sew each A section to a B section, matching seams. For block C, sew each A section to a B section and each C section to a D section. Sew the AB units to the CD units to complete the blocks. You should have four units for each block.

4. Arrange the units for block A into two horizontal rows of two units each. Sew the units in each row together, matching seams. Press the seam allowances open. Sew the rows together. Press the seam allowances open. Carefully remove the paper foundation. Repeat to make blocks B and C.

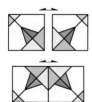

Block A

Block B

Block C

ASSEMBLING THE QUILT TOP

1. Alternately arrange the blocks and two black 2¾" x 6½" sashing rectangles into a vertical row. Sew the pieces together. Press the seam allowances open.

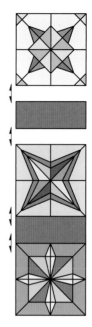

2. Refer to the quilt assembly diagram to sew the black 2¾" x 23" inner-border strips to the sides of the quilt top. Press the seam allowances open. Add the light-gray 5¾" x 23" outer-border strip to the right edge of the quilt top and the light-gray 2¾" x 23" outer-border strip to the left edge of the quilt top. Press the seam allowances open.

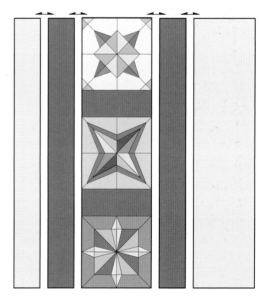

Quilt assembly

FINISHING THE QUILT

For help with any of the finishing techniques, go to ShopMartingale.com/HowtoQuilt to download free how-to information.

1. Layer the quilt top with backing and batting; baste the layers together.

2. Quilt as desired.

3. Bind the quilt edges using the black 2½"-wide strips.

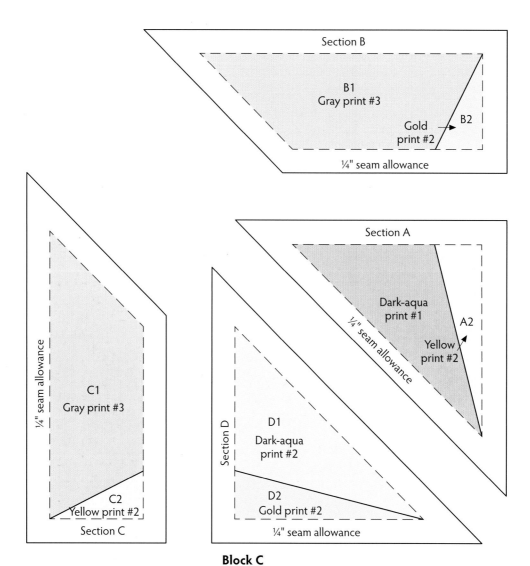

Section B

B1
Gray print #3

B2

Gold print #2

¼" seam allowance

Section A

Dark-aqua print #1

A2

Yellow print #2

¼" seam allowance

C1
Gray print #3

¼" seam allowance

C2
Yellow print #2

Section C

Section D

D1
Dark-aqua print #2

D2
Gold print #2

¼" seam allowance

Block C

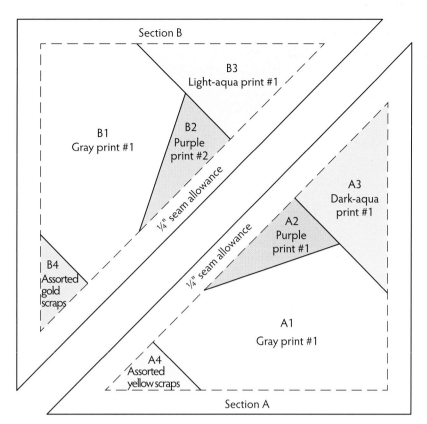

Block A

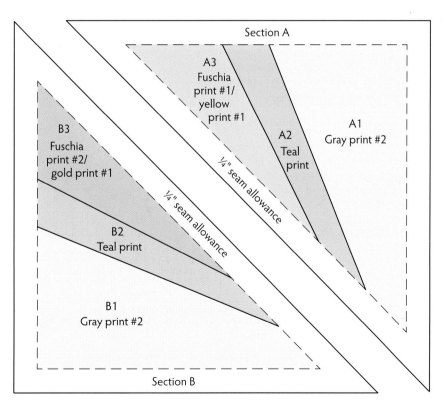

Block B

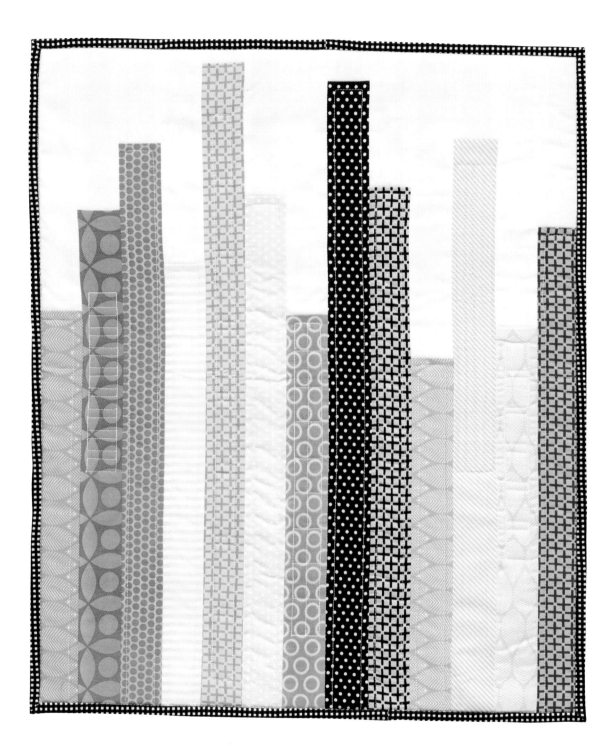

"Skyline," designed and made by Emily Herrick

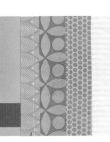

Skyline

FINISHED QUILT: 16¾" x 19½"

I may live in a small town now, but I'll always be a city girl at heart. With quick and easy piecing, this fun quilt lets you showcase a variety of colors and prints to create your own stunning skyline.

~Emily

MATERIALS

Yardage is based on 42"-wide fabric. Fat quarters are approximately 18" x 21".

13 strips of assorted bright prints, 1¾" wide and in lengths varying from 11" to 20"*

¼ yard of white solid for background

¼ yard of black polka dot for binding

⅝ yard of fabric for backing

19" x 22" piece of batting

Consult the cutting list for specific lengths.

CUTTING

From the white solid, cut:

2 strips, 1¾" x 42"; crosscut into:

　1 rectangle, 1¾" x 8½" (A)

　1 rectangle, 1¾" x 5½" (B)

　1 rectangle, 1¾" x 3½" (C)

　1 rectangle, 1¾" x 7" (D)

　1 rectangle, 1¾" x 1½" (E)

　1 rectangle, 1¾" x 4½" (F)

　1 rectangle, 1¾" x 8½" (G)

　1 rectangle, 1¾" x 2" (H)

　1 rectangle, 1¾" x 4½" (I)

　1 rectangle, 1¾" x 9½" (J)

　1 rectangle, 1¾" x 3" (K)

　1 rectangle, 1¾" x 8½" (L)

　1 rectangle, 1¾" x 5½" (M)

From the assorted-print strips, cut:

1 strip, 1¾" x 12" (A)

1 strip, 1¾" x 15" (B)

1 strip, 1¾" x 17" (C)

1 strip, 1¾" x 13½" (D)

1 strip, 1¾" x 19" (E)

1 strip, 1¾" x 16" (F)

1 strip, 1¾" x 12" (G)

1 strip, 1¾" x 18½" (H)

1 strip, 1¾" x 16" (I)

1 strip, 1¾" x 11" (J)

1 strip, 1¾" x 17½" (K)

1 strip, 1¾" x 12" (L)

1 strip, 1¾" x 15" (M)

From the black polka dot, cut:

2 strips, 2" x 42"

ASSEMBLING THE QUILT TOP

1. Referring to the letters in the cutting list, sew one end of each white rectangle to the end of the corresponding print strip. Press the seam allowances open. Mark each strip with its letter (see "Marking Fabric Pieces" below).

Marking Fabric Pieces

Emily suggests using a water-soluble pen to mark light-colored fabrics. Simply write the corresponding letter directly on the fabric to keep units in order. When the quilt is finished, give the letters a quick spritz of water and the marks completely disappear.

2. Refer to the quilt assembly diagram to arrange the pieced strips in alphabetical order from left to right. Sew the strips together, and press the seam allowances open.

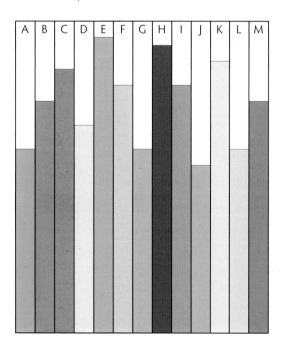

Quilt assembly

Sewing Multiple Strips

When sewing multiple strips together, Emily likes to alternate her sewing direction from one strip to the next to prevent skewing. To do this, she sews the strips together in pairs starting at the top. Then, when she sews the pairs together, she knows that the seams joining them should be sewn from the bottom upward.

FINISHING THE QUILT

For help with any of the finishing techniques, go to ShopMartingale.com/HowtoQuilt to download free how-to information.

1. Layer the quilt top with backing and batting; baste the layers together.

2. Quilt as desired.

3. Bind the quilt edges using the black 2"-wide strips.

Elongated Triangles

Love the look of traditional one-patch quilts but can't quite find the time for a full-size quilt? Make a mini! Slightly oversized and elongated patches take tradition a step ahead, and the small size is great for trying out improvisational piecing.

~Missy

MATERIALS

Yardage is based on 42"-wide fabric.

1 yard *total* of assorted solid and/or print scraps for triangles

¼ yard of dark-gray solid for binding

⅔ yard of fabric for backing

20" x 24" piece of batting

Template plastic

CUTTING

Before cutting the triangles for your quilt, refer to "Improvisational Piecing" below to make the pieced rectangles. Trace the triangle pattern on page 65 onto template plastic, transferring the dots; cut out the template and punch a small hole at each marked dot. Use the template to cut the triangles. After cutting the fabric triangles, transfer the dots to each one using a water-soluble pen.

From the assorted solids and/or prints and the pieced rectangles, cut:
54 triangles

From the dark-gray solid, cut:
2 strips, 2¼" x 42"

Improvisational Piecing

1. Place one scrap right side up on a cutting mat. Place a second scrap right side down on top of scrap 1. Align a rotary ruler along the overlapping edge of both pieces and trim the excess fabric. Sew along the trimmed edge, using a ¼" seam allowance. Press the seam allowances open.

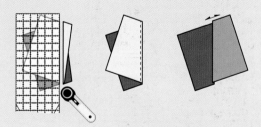

2. Repeat, adding additional scraps to make a pieced rectangle measuring approximately 5" x 7". Make nine pieced rectangles and cut a triangle shape from each using the pattern on page 65.

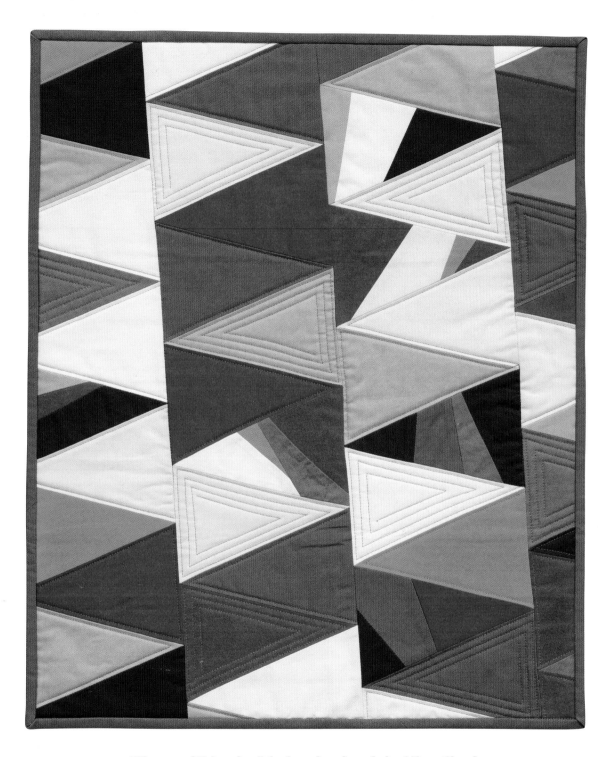

"Elongated Triangles," designed and made by Missy Shepler;
fabrics from the Soho Solids collection by Timeless Treasures

ASSEMBLING THE QUILT TOP

1. Refer to the quilt assembly diagram below to arrange the triangles in four horizontal rows, alternating the orientation of every other triangle. Row 1 has 13 triangles, row 2 has 14 triangles, row 3 has 14 triangles, and row 4 has 13 triangles.

2. With right sides together, join the triangles in each row along adjacent edges, making sure to match dots at the top and bottom edges on each triangle. Sew from dot to dot, backstitching at the dots. Press the seam allowances open.

Get the Point

Sew perfect points on your triangles. Place a pin perpendicular to the triangles, matching dots and aligning the tip of one triangle with the base of another. With the pin in place, align the adjacent edges, and pin the pieces together before sewing.

3. Join the rows. Note that the triangle points are offset between rows, and that row lengths are uneven. Press the seam allowances open.

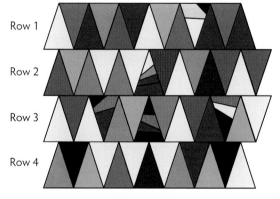

Row 1
Row 2
Row 3
Row 4

Quilt assembly

FINISHING THE QUILT

For help with any of the finishing techniques, go to ShopMartingale.com/HowtoQuilt to download free how-to information.

1. Layer the quilt top with backing and batting, arranging the quilt top at a slight angle; baste the layers together.

2. Quilt as desired. Trim the quilted piece to 18" x 22". Notice how Missy's quilt is trimmed off-kilter (not along the straight of grain) to give it even more of an improvisational look.

3. Bind the quilt edges using the gray 2¼"-wide strips.

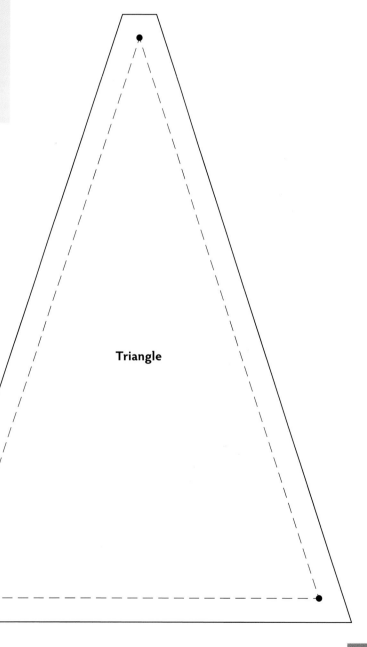

Triangle

"Stalagstripes," designed and made by Pippa Eccles Armbrester

Stalagstripes

FINISHED QUILT: 15½" x 19"

> Contemporary art provides me with a rich source of inspiration. This quilt is based on a print by Gary Andrew Clarke. I love the minimalist aesthetic and the way it's both simple and eye-catching. My sister thought up the name "stalagstripes" because the design reminded her of those magical cave formations.
>
> ~Pippa

MATERIALS

Yardage is based on 42"-wide fabric. Fat quarters measure approximately 18" x 21".

⅝ yard of off-white solid for background, border, and binding

Scraps, at least 1¾" x 7" *each*, of 14 assorted colorful solids for triangles

¼ yard or 1 fat quarter of black solid for triangles

1 fat quarter of fabric for backing

18" x 21" piece of batting

CUTTING

From *each* of the 14 colorful scraps, cut:
1 rectangle, 1¾" x 7" (14 total)

From the black solid, cut:
14 rectangles, 1¾" x 7"

From the off-white solid, cut:
1 rectangle, 9¼" x 20"
2 strips, 1½" x 42"
2 strips, 2" x 42"

MAKING THE TRIANGLES

1. Alternately sew four colored rectangles and three black rectangles together along the long edges to make a pieced rectangle. Press the seam allowances toward the black. Repeat to make a total of two striped rectangles. Make two additional striped rectangles in the same manner using four black and three colored rectangles. The striped rectangles should measure 7" x 9¼".

Make 2.   Make 2.

2. Make a mark 2" from the upper-left corner of each striped rectangle. Make another mark 4" from the initial mark. Mark the bottom edge 4" from the lower-left corner. Using your rotary cutter and ruler, cut two triangles from each striped rectangle as shown for a total of eight triangles.

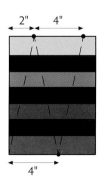

3. Mark the top and bottom edges of the white rectangle as shown, and then cut six triangles with a pointed tip and two triangles with a ½"-wide tip.

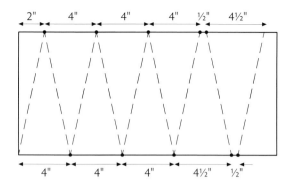

4. Cut the triangles with the ½"-wide tips in half lengthwise to make four half triangles.

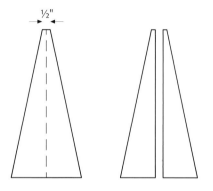

ASSEMBLING THE QUILT TOP

1. Lay out two striped rectangles with black points, two striped rectangles with colored points, and three full white triangles as shown. Sew the triangles together along the long edges. Press the seam allowances open. Add a half triangle to each end of the row. Press the seam allowances open. Repeat to make a total of two rows.

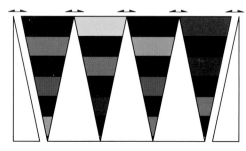

Make 2.

Piecing Triangles

The rows of triangles can be a tad finicky as you're sewing them together because the triangles are so skinny at the pointed ends. Just align the long edges of the triangles and sew an even ¼" seam allowance. Don't worry about cutting off any of the triangle; the seams will overlap at the tips. Sewing slowly will also help.

2. Sew the rows together, lining up the points of the striped triangles so they meet. Press the seam allowances open.

3. Measure the quilt top through the vertical center. From one of the white 1½" x 42" strips, cut two border strips to this measurement. Sew the strips to the sides of the quilt top. Press the seam allowances toward the border strips. Measure the quilt top through the horizontal center, including the border strips just added. From the remaining white 1½" x 42" strip, cut two border strips to this measurement. Sew the strips to the top and bottom of the quilt top. Press the seam allowances toward the border strips.

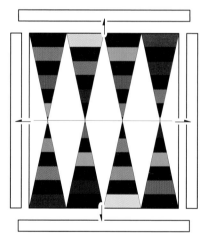

Quilt assembly

FINISHING THE QUILT

For help with any of the finishing techniques, go to ShopMartingale.com/HowtoQuilt to download free how-to information.

1. Layer the quilt top with backing and batting; baste the layers together.

2. Quilt as desired.

3. Bind the quilt edges using the white 2"-wide strips.

Perhaps

I've been interested in connecting quilts and codes for quite a while. Most of the time I use hidden codes to embed extremely direct messages in my quilts, but for this one I decided to go with something more ambiguous: the word *perhaps* translated into Morse code. That one word simultaneously embodies both possibility and skepticism; all that is needed to determine which way it leans is a subtle inflection of voice, or in this case the eye of the beholder.

~Thomas

MATERIALS

Yardage is based on 42"-wide fabric. Fat quarters measure approximately 18" x 21".

2½" x 42" strip *each* of red, yellow, blue, orange, green, and violet solids for pieced code

⅝ yard of tan linen blend for background and binding

⅔ yard of fabric for backing

20" x 24" piece of batting

CUTTING

From *each* of the red, yellow, and blue strips, cut:
1 square, 2½" x 2½" (3 total)
5 rectangles, 1½" x 2½" (15 total)
1 rectangle, 1½" x 4½" (3 total)

From the orange strip, cut:
1 square, 2½" x 2½"
6 rectangles, 1½" x 2½"
1 rectangle, 1½" x 4½"

From the green strip, cut:
1 square, 2½" x 2½"
6 rectangles, 1½" x 2½"

From the violet strip, cut:
1 square, 2½" x 2½"
3 rectangles, 1½" x 2½"
2 rectangles, 1½" x 4½"

From the tan linen, cut:
6 strips, 1½" x 42"; crosscut into:
    8 strips, 1½" x 17½"
    19 rectangles, 1½" x 2½"
4 strips, 2½" x 42"; crosscut 2 *of the strips* into:
    1 rectangle, 2½" x 3½"
    4 rectangles, 2½" x 4½"
    2 rectangles, 2½" x 5½"
    1 rectangle, 2½" x 6½"
    1 rectangle, 2½" x 11½"

"Perhaps," designed and made by Thomas Knauer

MAKING THE PIECED UNITS

1. Sew two 2½" squares together side by side to make the color combinations shown. Make one of each color combination. Press the seam allowances toward the darker square of each pair.

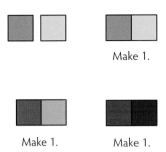

Make 1.

Make 1.   Make 1.

2. Sew two 1½" x 2½" rectangles together along the long edges to make the color combinations shown. Make the number of units indicated for each color combination. Press the seam allowances toward the darker rectangle of each pair.

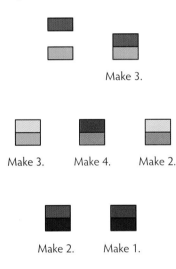

Make 3.

Make 3.   Make 4.   Make 2.

Make 2.   Make 1.

3. Sew two 1½" x 4½" rectangles together along the long edges to make the color combinations shown. Make the number of units indicated for each color combination. Press the seam allowances toward the darker rectangle of each pair.

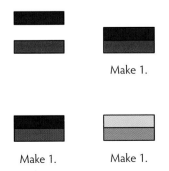

Make 1.

Make 1.   Make 1.

ASSEMBLING THE QUILT TOP

1. Refer to the quilt assembly diagram to arrange the pieced units and tan rectangles into seven rows. Sew the pieces in each row together. Press the seam allowances toward the tan rectangles.

2. Alternately sew the tan 1½" x 17½" strips and pieced rows together as shown. Press the seam allowances toward the tan strips.

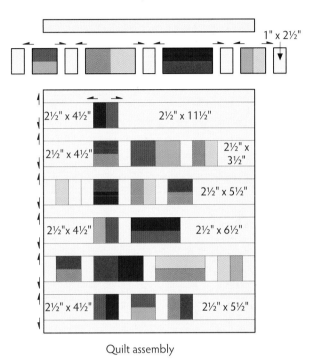

Quilt assembly

FINISHING THE QUILT

For help with any of the finishing techniques, go to ShopMartingale.com/HowtoQuilt to download free how-to information.

1. Layer the quilt top with backing and batting; baste the layers together.

2. Quilt as desired. Thomas quilted lines that radiated from the bottom-left corner as a reference to the transmission of a signal.

3. Bind the quilt edges using the tan 2½"-wide strips.

"Particularly Joyful," designed and made by Victoria L. Eapen;
fabrics from the Curio collection by Basic Grey for Moda

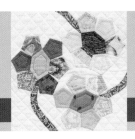

Particularly Joyful

I've always been inspired by the color wheel. Fabric arranged as the color wheel is particularly joyful. When I was beginning this appliqué project, I picked up one of my fat-eighth fabric bundles that had been aging appropriately for a few months. It was arranged in that familiar color wheel of inspiration, and I thought, what better way to use an entire collection than by making flowers? I hope you'll be inspired to pick up a bundle of fabric that's been aging on your shelf and give these petals a try.

~Vickie

MATERIALS

Yardage is based on 42"-wide fabric. Fat quarters measure approximately 18" x 21"; fat eighths measure approximately 9" x 21".

1 fat eighth *each* of 39 assorted florals for flower appliqués and pieced outer border

½ yard of white print for appliqué background and middle border

⅜ yard of yellow print for inner border and binding

1 fat quarter of brown floral for stem appliqués

⅔ yard of fabric for backing

22" x 26" piece of batting

½" bias-tape maker (optional)

CUTTING

From the white print, cut:
1 strip, 14½" x 42"; crosscut into:
    1 square, 12½" x 12½"
    2 strips, 2½" x 14½"

From 36 of the assorted floral fat eighths, cut:
1 rectangle, 1½" x 9" (36 total)

From the *bias* of the brown floral, cut:
3 strips, 1" x 20"

From the yellow print, cut:
2 strips, 1½" x 42"; crosscut into:
    2 strips, 1½" x 14½"
    2 strips, 1½" x 12½"
3 strips, 2¼" x 42"

APPLIQUÉING THE CENTER BLOCK AND BORDER STRIPS

1. Fold the white 12½" square in half diagonally in both directions. Finger-press the folds to mark the center. Fold the white 2½" x 14½" strips in half horizontally and vertically; finger-press the folds to mark the center.

2. Using your favorite appliqué method and the patterns on page 75, prepare the large and small flower centers and petals from the fabrics indicated on the patterns. Make the number of pieces indicated for each shape.

Try English Paper Piecing

Vickie basted her flower fabrics to paper templates using the English paper piecing method. The paper helped stabilize the fabric, allowing her to sew the petals to the flower centers before appliquéing the flowers to the background fabric. The great thing about appliqué is that any appliqué method will work—the best method is one that *you* enjoy.

3. Using a ½" bias-tape maker or the bias-tape method of your choice, make ½"-wide finished vines from the brown 1" x 20" bias strips.

4. Referring to the placement guide below and the quilt photo (page 72), position the large flower centers, large flower petals, and stems on the white square so that the design is centered. Appliqué the pieces in place using your desired method.

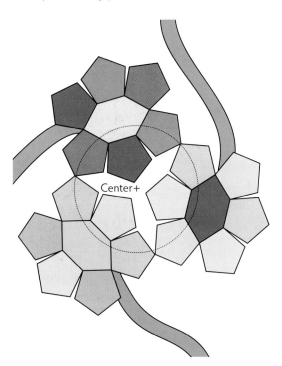

Center block appliqué placement

5. Referring to the border placement guide below and the quilt photo, position the small flower centers and small flower petals on the white middle-border strips. Appliqué the pieces in place.

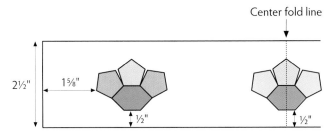

Border appliqué placement

MAKING THE OUTER-BORDER UNITS

1. Randomly select two floral 1½" x 9" rectangles and sew them together along the long edges to make a strip set. Press the seam allowances open. Repeat to make a total of 18 strip sets. Crosscut the strip sets into 72 segments, 1½" wide.

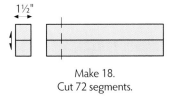

Make 18.
Cut 72 segments.

2. Randomly select two segments and sew them together to make a four-patch unit. Press the seam allowances open. Repeat to make a total of 36 units.

ASSEMBLING THE QUILT TOP

1. Refer to the quilt assembly diagram to sew the yellow 1½" x 12½" inner-border strips to the sides of the appliquéd block. Press the seam allowances toward the border strips. Sew the yellow 1½" x 14½" inner-border strips to the top and bottom of the block. Press the seam allowances toward the border strips.

2. Join the appliquéd middle-border strips to the top and bottom of the quilt top. Press the seam allowances toward the inner border.

3. Sew nine four-patch units together side by side to make an outer-border strip. Press the seam allowances open. Repeat to make a total of four strips.

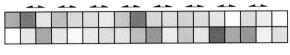

Make 4.

4. Sew two pieced outer-border strips to the sides of the quilt top. Press the seam allowances toward the outer border. Sew the remaining two pieced outer-border strips to the top and bottom of the quilt top. Press the seam allowances toward the outer border.

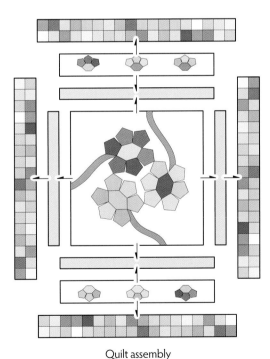

Quilt assembly

FINISHING THE QUILT

For help with any of the finishing techniques, go to ShopMartingale.com/HowtoQuilt to download free how-to information.

1. Layer the quilt top with backing and batting; baste the layers together.

2. Quilt as desired.

3. Bind the quilt edges using the yellow 2¼"-wide strips.

Appliqué patterns do not include seam allowances.

Small flower center

Make 6 from assorted florals.

Small flower petal

Make 6 sets of 3 coordinating from assorted florals.

Large flower center
Make 3 from assorted florals.

1"

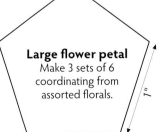

Large flower petal
Make 3 sets of 6 coordinating from assorted florals.

1"

"Woven Stars," pieced and made by Rebecca Silbaugh

Woven Stars

There's nothing more timeless than stars created from scrappy, simple pieces. This small quilt just happens to use those stars in a more creative way. I couldn't wait to break into my stash to make this quilt!

~Rebecca

MATERIALS

Yardage is based on 42"-wide fabric. Fat quarters are approximately 18" x 21".

32 squares, 2½" x 2½", of assorted light fabrics

24 squares, 3" x 3", of assorted light fabrics

12 squares, 3" x 3", of assorted medium fabrics

12 squares, 3" x 3", of assorted dark fabrics

¼ yard of brown stripe for binding

1 fat quarter of fabric for backing

20" x 24" piece of batting

CUTTING

From the brown stripe, cut:
2 strips, 2¼" x 42"

MAKING THE BLOCKS

1. Draw a diagonal line from corner to corner on the wrong side of each light 3" square. Place a marked square on each medium and dark 3" square, right sides together. Stitch ¼" from both sides of the marked line. Cut the squares apart on the marked line to make a total of 48 units. Press the seam allowances open. Trim each half-square-triangle unit to 2½" x 2½".

Make 24. Make 24.

2. Arrange six dark half-square-triangle units, four medium half-square-triangle units, and six light 2½" squares into four horizontal rows of four pieces each as shown, paying careful attention to the positioning of the half-square-triangle units. Sew the pieces in each row together. Press the seam allowances open. Sew the rows together. Press the seam allowances open. Repeat to make a total of four blocks.

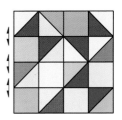 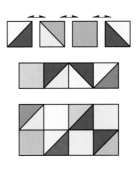

Make 4.

ASSEMBLING THE QUILT TOP

1. Arrange the blocks into two horizontal rows of two blocks each, rotating the blocks as shown to create the pattern. Sew the blocks in each row together. Press the seam allowances open. Sew the rows together. Press the seam allowances open.

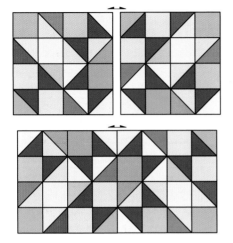

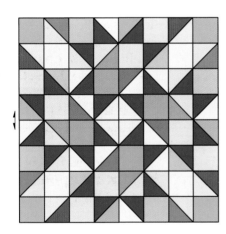

2. Join four medium half-square-triangle units and four light 2½" squares into a horizontal row, rotating the half-square-triangle units as shown. Press the seam allowances open. Repeat to make a total of two border strips.

Make 2.

3. Sew the border strips to the top and bottom of the quilt top as shown. Press the seam allowances open.

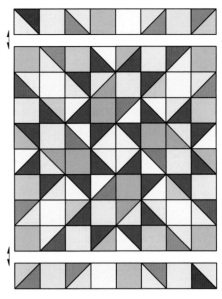

Quilt assembly

FINISHING THE QUILT

For help with any of the finishing techniques, go to ShopMartingale.com/HowtoQuilt to download free how-to information.

1. Layer the quilt top with backing and batting; baste the layers together.

2. Quilt as desired.

3. Bind the quilt edges using the brown 2¼"-wide strips.

About the Contributors

Pippa Eccles Armbrester

Pippa is a full-time quilter living and working in Boston. Her work focuses on solid fabrics and bold geometry, patterns that balance the tradition of quilting and patchwork with a contemporary aesthetic. She has a fuss-free and joyful attitude toward the quiltmaking process and creates quilts that are meant to be used and loved. Pippa enjoys travel, cooking, and baking (especially bread). Knitting and crochet are her portable needleworks of choice. Check out her website, PippaQuilts.com.

Jeni Baker

Jeni loves to find ways to be creative every day, whether through photography, sewing, or quilting. She's been sewing since she was 11 years old. In addition to designing sewing and quilting patterns, she designs fabric for Art Gallery Fabrics. In her spare time, Jeni enjoys collecting vintage kitchenware and spending time with her pet bunny, George. To learn more about Jeni and her quilting adventures, visit her blog, InColorOrder.com.

Natalie Barnes

Natalie is the owner and designer for beyond the reef, a pattern-design company that she started in 1994 while drinking coffee on a lanai in Hanalei, Kauai. As a little girl, she learned to sew, knit, and crochet from her grandmother, and later began quilting with 99-cent Woolworth fabrics. After a successful career in the demanding commercial interior-design field in Los Angeles, Natalie decided it was time to live her dream and put her talents to work in another field. Having always lived on the beach, her inspiration for color and design comes from the sea, the sky, and the land. You can visit Natalie at beyondthereefpatterns.com.

Melissa Corry

Melissa started quilting as a casual hobby about 10 years ago, but in the last few years she's been drawn in hook, line, and sinker. Starting a quilting blog seemed like the natural thing to do to share her passion. She never would have guessed her blog would lead to creating her own designs, as well as tutorials, published works, and even a pattern line. Melissa loves designing and finds inspiration in just about everything and anything. Melissa, her husband, and their five little children live in Cedar City, Utah. To see more of her daily quilting adventures, check out her blog, Happy Quilting, at HappyQuiltingMelissa. blogspot.com.

Elizabeth Dackson

Elizabeth fell in love with quilting as a way to regain her sanity while her son entered the terrible twos. Her first quilting book, *Becoming a Confident Quilter* (Martingale, 2013), is full of tips, exercises, and skill-building quilt patterns. Additional quilt designs can be found on her blog, Don't Call Me Betsy (DontCallMeBetsy.com), as well as in various quilting publications. A founding member of the Tampa Modern Quilt Guild, Elizabeth lives in Florida with her husband, son, and neurotic beagle.

Victoria L. Eapen

Vickie was born and raised in Dubuque, Iowa. Creativity has played a part of her entire life. Inspired by her mother, at age eight she began her first sewing class. The first project was a pink dotted-Swiss skirt. Through Vickie's school-aged years, home-economics sewing led to interests in counted cross-stitch, crochet taught by her great-grandmother, and knitting. She was bitten by the quilting

bug in 1997 and remains passionate for the art. In 2005 she started a blog, SpunSugarQuilt.com, where she shares tutorials and patterns. Her other patterns and projects can be found online, in quilting magazines, and in her book, *Large-Block Quilts* (Martingale, 2013). When she's not blogging or quilting, Vickie is a full-time dentist in Ashland, Ohio, where she resides with her husband of 15 years, two beautiful daughters, and three cats.

Debbie Grifka

Making quilts with clean lines and bold shapes is what Debbie loves best, whether the colors are deep and intense or low-contrast neutrals. Debbie's work has been displayed at both Paducah and Houston and featured in various magazines and books. The main focus of her work is her pattern business, Esch House Quilts. Debbie blogs at EschHouseQuilts.com and is active on several social-media sites. She is vice president of the Ann Arbor (Michigan) Modern Quilt Guild and a member of the Greater Ann Arbor Quilt Guild.

Julie Herman

Julie is better known in the quilting community as Jaybird, a childhood nickname. She is the author of the best-selling book *Skip the Borders,* also published by Martingale (2012), and her quilts have appeared in numerous quilting magazines. Julie has an extensive quilt-pattern line, Jaybird Quilts, as well as a line of her own unique quilting rulers, including the Hex N More, Mini Hex N More, and Sidekick rulers. Her website, JaybirdQuilts.com, has a robust content offering, with free tutorials and an active blog. Her motto is "One girl on a mission to make life better with fabric!"

Emily Herrick

Emily lives in Utah with her husband, Gilbert, and their children, Preston, Logan, and Paris. She began her creative journey at a young age, drawing on her bedroom walls. Thankfully her talent has taken a much more productive turn. Dabbling in the "crafty" arts most of her life, she started a quilt-pattern company in 2006 under the name Crazy Old Ladies. In 2011 she joined the team at Michael Miller Fabrics, LLC, as a licensed fabric designer. In 2012 she self-published her first eBook. Visit Emily's blog, CrazyOldLadiesQuilts.blogspot.com.

Kimberly Jolly

Kimberly is the owner of Fat Quarter Shop, an online fabric store, and It's Sew Emma, a pattern company. Kimberly has been quilting for more than 15 years and her designs are mainly inspired by vintage quilts and blocks, but she occasionally ventures out to try something fresh and new. Kimberly loves to create quilts for friends and family, especially her children, who are a constant source of inspiration.

Thomas Knauer

Thomas holds master of fine arts degrees from both Ohio University and the Cranbrook Academy of Art. Before he started designing fabric and quilts, he was a professor of art and design at Drake University and the State University of New York. He began sewing in 2010 after leaving academia; the first time he sat down at a sewing machine he made his wee daughter a dress. Thomas has designed fabric with Andover Fabrics and his first book has just been published. He still loves making things for his children.

Cheri Leffler

Cheri lives in Helotes, Texas, with her husband of 29 years. Even though all four of their daughters have grown up and left home for either college or careers, Cheri confesses to still struggling to find enough hours in the day! She has only been designing for a few years, but happily, ideas just come faster than her fingers can fly. You can see more of her designs at CheriLefflerDesigns.com.

Missy Shepler

Whenever possible, Missy combines her "day job" as a designer, author, and illustrator with her love of stitching by creating projects, patterns, and illustrations for sewing and quilting clients and publications. See more of Missy's designs, including a peek at past publications, at MissyStitches.com.

Rebecca Silbaugh

Rebecca is a creative soul with a passion for quilting. It hasn't always been that way, but when a career in graphic design wasn't what she expected, her focus turned to all of the yummy fabrics at her mom's quilt shop. From that moment, she became a quilter and opened Ruby Blue Quilting Studio in 2009. Rebecca is the author of *Seamingly Scrappy* (Martingale, 2013) and loves any excuse to create scrap quilts. When she's not at home quilting and playing with her dogs, Rebecca can be found traveling with her husband, Ben, but you can always find her on her blog at RubyBlueQuilts.blogspot.com.

Jocelyn Ueng

Jocelyn is the design director for It's Sew Emma, a pattern company. She claims to be a novice quilter, but having worked in the quilting world for several years has changed the way she looks at all things. Jocelyn loves to extract designs from her surroundings and her biggest emphasis is on versatility of design. She wants others—no matter their taste—to be able to use her designs and make them into original pieces to be loved.

Heather Valentine

Heather is the creative juice behind the Sewing Loft, a sewing community focused on inspiring sewists to reclaim their creativity, one stitch at a time. After earning a degree in fashion design and pattern making from New York's Fashion Institute of Technology, Heather took her talent to some of the top name brands in the apparel industry and is now a pattern designer for Simplicity Patterns. You can find her sharing her creative process and sewing tips on her blog, TheSewingLoft.com.

Jackie White

Jackie is a mother of two young boys and married to a wonderful guy. Her passion is creating three-dimensional art quilts and she teaches workshops and gives lectures and trunk shows on her three-dimensional techniques. Her work has been juried into shows across North America. She also writes for two publications, one being a humorous column on quilting. When she's not in her studio (which is packed with embellishments!), you can find her at her blog at JabotQuilt.blogspot.ca.